Law in Civil Society

Law in Civil Society

Richard Dien Winfield

 University Press of Kansas

Published by the University Press of Kansas (Lawrence, Kansas 66049), which was organized by the Kansas Board of Regents and is operated and funded by Emporia State University, Fort Hays State University, Kansas State University, Pittsburg State University, the University of Kansas, and Wichita State University

Library of Congress Cataloging-in-Publication Data

Winfield, Richard Dien, 1950–
     Law in civil society / Richard Dien Winfield.
        p.   cm.
     Includes index.
        ISBN 0-7006-0698-X (cloth : alk. paper)   ISBN 0-7006-0699-8 (pbk. : alk. paper)
     1. Law—Philosophy.   2. Civil society.   I. Title.
     K230.W54L39   1995
     340′.1—dc20   94-42829

British Library Cataloguing in Publication Data is available.

Printed in the United States of America

10 9 8 7 6 5 4 3 2 1

The paper used in this publication meets the minimum requirements of the American National Standard for Permanence of Paper for Printed Library Materials Z39.48-1984.

For my son, Rasik Sidd

Contents

Acknowledgments

Law in Civil Society attempts to complete the theory of civil society whose other portions I developed in outline in *The Just Economy* (New York: Routledge, 1988).

My essay, "Freedom from Foundations: The Normativity of Autonomy in Theory and Practice," which appeared in the *Jadavpur Journal of Philosophy* 4: 1 (Fall 1992): 1–27, is incorporated in slightly altered form in Chapter 1.

Material published separately as "Rethinking the Legal Process," *American Journal of Jurisprudence* 39 (December 1994), is contained with minor alterations in Chapter 6.

Introduction:
Law and Freedom

The Bias of the Philosophy of Law

Taken as a discrete discipline, the philosophy of law presents a puzzle. It presumes to address a topic sufficiently unitary and independent to warrant a theory of its own, just as any positive science turns to its object as something whose distinct identity first allows for its investigation. Yet legal philosophy can proceed in this way solely if it truncates its own understanding by presupposing the normative neutrality of law. Only when the concept of law is assumed to be independent of all norms applying to the domains of its jurisdiction can legality be conceived apart from a far more encompassing investigation of ethics. Otherwise, the rights and duties of other spheres will dictate what kind of rules law should uphold and how legal practice should function, enjoining legal inquiry to examine every facet of justice in order to determine the form and content of law.

Not surprisingly, the thinkers who have developed independent philosophies of law are primarily legal positivists and communitarians. Although legal positivists may acknowledge that legality stipulates and enforces a system of norms, they suppose that law has a ubiquitous, conceptually determinable structure independent of any particular ethical system. Communitarians, for their part, may admit that legality operates only in a community whose members act in recognition of shared values endowing legal norms with authority, but they assume that any ethical considerations shaping law are rooted in communal practices that are historical conventions inscrutable to reason. Either way, legal philosophy becomes a formal science for which issues of justice drop out as extraneous variables, leaving the concept of law an empty scaffold applying indifferently to competing ethical systems.

By contrast, those theorists who choose to think about law without making such assumptions find the philosophy of law an unwieldy enterprise. If law falls within ethics, then an investigation of legality that restricts its view to legal practice can treat only the pertinent norms that define the scope and form of law as independently determined givens, whose systematic account must fall beyond the limits of the philosophy of law into the wider reach of the philosophy of right. In that case, the practitioners of legal philosophy become the poor cousins of practical philosophers, depending on the latter for a guidance and direction they need but cannot themselves supply. If, however, a serious attempt is made to investigate the structures of right that may determine what law should prescribe and how law should be enacted and executed, the theory of law relinquishes its discrete character and becomes subsumed within the system of ethics. In that case, the content and parameters of legal practice can be established only in conjunction with conceiving the normative dimension of property relations, morality, the family, society, and the state. It is therefore no accident that those thinkers who have attributed ethical worth to law have not provided separate doctrines of law but have instead treated legal affairs in scattered recesses of their practical philosophies.

This situation testifies to how the whole discipline of the "philosophy of law" is necessarily slanted from the start. Only by adopting a normatively indifferent stance can one entertain law as a discrete object of investigation warranting separate study. Yet such study cannot count as the general field it pretends to be, for it represents only a particular approach to law and excludes others.

Freedom and the Normativity of Law

Among those thinkers who have affirmed the ethical dimension of law and accordingly refrained from developing a discrete legal philosophy, there is a recurring recognition that law's normativity is tied to its relation to freedom. Although ancient and modern theorists may disagree on how exclusively the justice of law rests upon this relation, few would deny that a good life, a community of free individuals, and legality are all intertwined.

At first glance, any such connection might appear ludicrous insofar as freedom, commonsensically understood as the exercise of free choice, seems at odds with any submission to law. This very discrepancy may be thought to give law its mandate, for if what is right has its measure in rules laid down by nature, convention, or reason independently of the wills subject to them, then the enactment and enforcement of such rules will be required to curb the license of free choice. Yet again and again, law has been understood as both a condition for freedom and an ingredient in its realization. Moreover, freedom, far from being opposed to what is ethical, has been ever more recognized as the substance of right. With normative validity increasingly perceived to reside in freedom, law's intimate connection with autonomy has come to be seen as the source of authority for legality.

What, then, is the connection between law and freedom? The answer to this question naturally depends upon what is meant by law and by freedom. Of particular concern is whether legality be understood as government under law or rule by law and whether freedom be construed as what is commonly distinguished as negative or positive freedom. Accordingly, law's tie to freedom can be set into a preliminary focus by first considering the implications of these divergent, albeit complementary interpretations.[1]

Freedom and Rule under Law

Government under law, or constitutionality, as it has come to be understood in an age of constitutionalism, is traditionally recognized to be a bulwark of liberty, protecting legal subjects from the arbitrariness and bias of personal rule. By subjecting all citizens, rulers and ruled alike, to the impersonal dominion of a sovereign law, government under law might well be said, paraphrasing Cicero, to make all citizens free to the degree that they are slaves to the law.[2]

Nevertheless, unless law is automatically fair or, failing that, a legislator can be found who cannot help but be impartial, the rule of law can secure such freedom from personal domination only if there is a core of laws fundamentally immune from enactment or repeal by any of the individuals subject to them. Solely when the ruling laws comprise a nonamendable constitution given antecedently to its citizenry could law then offer a firm barrier against the impositions of personal rule by a particular agent or group of agents.

Yet even in this case, government under law will not be a dispassionate and impartial buffer against individual license unless the content of constitutional law is itself free of bias. Since this content may reflect who has founded the constitution, it may well be said that the rule of law will be fair provided the founders of the state are concerned with the common good. Even then, however, the freedom from personal arbitrariness that the primacy of law can offer may still involve subjection to rules completely obstructing autonomy, unless the common good leaves room for liberty.

Accordingly, if rule under law is to have any connection with freedom, even a freedom so minimally construed as the noninterference with personal liberty, then the content of law must be appropriately restricted, either by locating founders or legislators who can be counted on to will the proper law or by conceiving what law should be and hoping that it has been or will be realized, if not by statute, then by the precedents or customs of common law.

Freedom and Rule by Law

Rule by law might appear to have a more intimate bond to freedom than rule under law. Although these two dimensions of law commonly go together, they are by no means inseparable. In a constitutional state, government officials who execute the law, either as judges who apply the law to particular cases, or as bureaucrats who implement legislative and judicial decisions, operate under the rule of law without doing so by means of law. For although their actions are governed by law, their lawful role in governing does not consist in legislating. Conversely, those who found the constitution, the constituent legislators, act by law but not under law.[3] For although they mandate the fundamental law of the state, their institution of constitutional government cannot be subject to any law if the constitution is itself to be the ultimate measure of legality. Only legislators within a constitutional state actually exercise power both by and under law, since their enactment of positive law proceeds within a framework ordained not by their own legislation but by constitutional statute. Significantly, it is this legislative function that is given primacy within the modern constitutional state,[4] for which freedom is supposed to play so central a role. Does this conjuncture signify that law achieves its marriage with freedom when rule under law gets combined with rule by law?

Certainly, the value of rule by law does indeed closely complement the value of rule under law. Whereas rule under law serves to hold in check the arbitrariness and partiality of rule by individuals, rule by law has the virtue of supplanting ad hoc decrees and custom with standing abstract norms applying equally to all legal subjects.[5] By exercising power through standing abstract norms made public to those to whom they are addressed, rule by law provides security to individuals, who can know in advance which types of action are prescribed or prohibited as well as what responses to expect from government.[6] Such predictability depends upon two features: the public durability of legal enactment, by which the law remains in force until it is repealed, and the abstraction of legal statute, which always commands conditions to be subscribed to in acting, rather than particular performances.[7] Rule by law thus represents a benefit that cannot be offered by rule by decree, which commands a particular individual or group to perform specific actions whose execution exhausts the force of the decree, leaving open what performances will next be expected.[8] Similarly, by imposing general norms applying to all legal subjects alike, rule by law affords individuals an equal treatment by government that cannot be guaranteed by rule by decree, even when such decree stands under law. Although the content of laws may entail an uneven distribution of benefits as a result of their application, in respect to form, rule by law excludes any direct privileging or denigrating of particular individuals.[9]

Yet, if rule by law entails the security of being beholden to standing, publicly promulgated rules, as well as equal treatment by government, does this security carry with it any enhancement of freedom? Legal subjects may know what kinds of activities are mandated by standing laws, but does the question not remain whether these laws are rules that impugn autonomy? By the same token, the generality of law may entail equal treatment of all legal subjects, but could this equality be just as well the vehicle of a shared bondage?

Although the security provided by the abstractness, continuous applicability, and publicity of rule by law says little about what freedom of action it extends to individuals, it has been recognized to comprise a necessary, if not sufficient condition for the exercise of rights of any sort. Without a consistent application and enforcement of standing laws[10] letting individuals know which sort of actions are legally upheld or prohibited, the boundaries of liberty become uncertain, leaving individuals unsure of their rights and duties, as well as deprived of any abiding, consistent enforcement of their freedoms.[11]

In addition, the abstract character of rule by law automatically leaves to the individual a dimension of free discretion upon which depends the fulfillment of legal command. To some extent, this element of discretion is inherent in following any commands, whether decrees that order particular individuals to perform a specific act at a certain time and place or statutes that set general guidelines for conduct. Whereas custom and habit may determine the particular detail of the actions of an individual and do so without having been consciously apprehended by that agent, a command is expressly fulfilled on the condition of being made known to the commanded agent and by being realized through an act of will that adds its own contribution to the particular manner in which the command is executed.[12] In this respect, every command exhibits two cardinal features entailed in rule by law: obtaining realization by being object to the understanding of the agent and manifesting a generality involving a distinction between the essence of what is commanded and the details of its execution. Owing to the latter abstractness inherent in any command, the agent can obey by not just understanding it, but taking an initiative in determining exactly how it will be fulfilled. If the act in question were exhaustively specified independently of such initiative, it would no longer be obedience to a command but rather comprise the rote action of a tool or machine, where an operator directly controls an instrument. Thus, obedience to command, whether decree or law, entails an act of freedom on the part of the agent, an act that consists not simply in the will to submit but in the will to determine what is not yet given in the understood content of the command.[13]

The abstractness of rule by law, however, is not limited to the generality of command. By comprising a rule mandating a type of action to legal subjects in general, rule by law calls for a compliance involving a wider initiative than that simply bridging the gap between the essence of an order and the indifferent detail of its execution. Because law

commands conditions to be subscribed to in acting rather than achievements of particular ends,[14] legal subjects enjoy a freedom to determine
what they will that subjects of decree do not.

Yet how substantial are the freedoms inherent in the objectivity and
generality of rule by law? The public objectivity of law may indeed
leave legal subjects free of any immediate control by government,[15]
making understanding of the law a condition of its realization by each
individual in addition to providing knowledge of what rights and duties are legally enforced. Conversely, the abstractness of law may give
each legal subject the prerogative of deciding precisely what actions to
take in abiding by legal statutes. Nevertheless, without further restrictions upon the content of legislation, do these features prevent legality
from restricting the autonomy of individuals to an empty formality?

"Negative" Freedom and Law

It might seem that by involving rule under and by law, legality would
automatically safeguard "negative" freedom, understood as the liberty
to pursue ends of one's own choosing that do not interfere with other
people doing the same. In virtue of the primacy of law over government, legality could be thought to protect individuals from unwarranted interference, just as in virtue of the objectivity and generality
of law, legality could be taken to preserve the prerogatives of personal
liberty from external encroachment. This seems particularly true if the
abstractness of legal statute entails that all law consists in prohibitions
rather than positive precepts.[16] Whatever legal acts individuals under-
take would then be expressions of private initiative.

Law, however, can preside over government and comprise a published code of rules yet still restrict personal liberties in ways that have
little to do with bringing harmony to the private pursuits of legal
subjects. Rule under and by law can just as well impede personal
disposition over property as confine the movements of individuals.
Negative freedom can be linked to legality only if law is defined as the
system of norms enabling the freedom of choice of individuals to
coexist according to universal rules, a Kantian definition characteristic
of the liberal tradition. This definition, however, reflects not the form
of law per se, but a substantive commitment concerning the content of

legal statute, a commitment that excludes from consideration any legislation channeling conduct independently of what protects private affairs from outside interference.[17]

"Positive" Freedom and Law

The tie between the institutional rights of "positive" freedom and law is similarly conditional. If we follow the argument of Rousseau, which Kant later adopts, it might seem that rule under and by law is inextricably bound up with an institutional freedom in which all legal subjects participate. Whereas in submitting to the personal rule of another an individual is unfree, in obeying law one is subject to a public will that is as much one's own as anyone else's. Hence, compliance with law is not a restriction of freedom but a realization of the autonomy that consists in complying with self-imposed rules whose enforcement is publicly guaranteed. Unlike the liberty of negative freedom, this autonomy can only be enjoyed under conditions of legality. Yet, as both Rousseau and Kant acknowledge, the autonomy in question is not in play when law is a common law based on custom or judicial precedent or when law is decreed by a legislator, however enlightened, whose will is something distinct from that of the individuals subject to it. Although, as Rousseau maintains, the generality of law may make it universal in application, obedience to law will not be the form of political self-determination by which one submits to laws of which one is coauthor unless law emanates from a general will, comprising a legislature in which all legal subjects participate. Accordingly, law is not tied to such positive freedom unless one invokes a political doctrine of direct democracy, a doctrine quite independent of the concept of law.[18]

By the same token, law cannot be tied to such nonpolitical positive freedoms as the autonomy of market agency or that of membership in a free family unless the content of law be restricted in view of what is specific to these modes of association. Admittedly, the laws of the market can operate only if civil law protects property entitlements and leaves individuals free to choose what to buy and sell and what occupation to seek.[19] Nonetheless, economic autonomy can just as well be undercut by laws of different ambitions, such as those operating in states that have supplanted market institutions with public enterprise controlled by central economic planning.

Similarly, individuals may only be able to exercise the freedom to choose marriage partners, raise natural or adopted children as they see fit within the limits of "responsible parenthood," and divorce by mutual agreement on the condition that civil law refrains from mandating independent procedures for organizing families and childrearing. Yet law could just as easily prescribe alternate arrangements as diverse as collectivized households and caste systems. All these arrangements could be made to fit the general form of a legal norm. For despite law's abstractness and universal application, it can involve rules that divide individuals according to clan, race, religion, or any other factor that can be specified in general, as the "separate but equal" legal façades of apartheid and Jim Crow America have made notorious.

Accordingly, if freedom is to be the substance of legitimacy, and the authority of law is to be sought in its connection to self-determination, the content of law and legal practice will apparently have to be subject to restrictions derived from independent ethical considerations. Rule under and by law may be necessary conditions for the exercise of different forms of autonomy, yet neither negative nor positive freedoms seem to derive sufficient support from legality without molding law in conformity to extralegal prescriptions.

Accordingly, even when the normativity of law is sought in its inherent connection with freedom, a formal treatment of legality will not suffice. As long as law is treated as a phenomenon existing apart, with a nature undefined by other spheres of right, legality will be an empty scaffold, indifferent to the concrete features of self-determination by which law can alone command its due authority. This abiding qualification in law's relation to freedom confronts legal philosophy with the need to conceive law in the context of the spheres of right, drawing upon the concepts of the different modes of freedom and determining how law must enter the constitution of their reality. Only thus can law's contribution to the institutions of freedom be assessed. Granted that normativity in conduct is one with the reality of self-determination, what law should be can be determined only by developing law in this context of the spheres of right.[20]

In order to justify investigating law in the context of the institutions of right, however, the normativity of freedom cannot simply be accepted as a cultural given of modernity or as the theoretical predilection of our most admired thinkers. The exclusive legitimacy of self-determination must first be established in its own right.

1 • The Normativity of Freedom

The Problem of Foundations in Theory and Practice

The fate of freedom stands very much at a crossroads.[1] On the one hand, the call for self-determination has gathered renewed momentum, penetrating all spheres of conduct. At the most rudimentary level of right, the entitlement of ownership has been claimed for all rational agents, excluding slavery once and for all. At the level of moral reflection, the right to an independent conscience has gained ever-widening ground, freeing personal conduct from the yoke of elders, clergy, and all other privileged authority. In the household, the family has become increasingly liberated from external restraints that prevent adults from marrying whom they wish and from freely comanaging household affairs, irrespective of race, caste, nationality, religion, and, most recently, gender and sexual preference. At the social plane, the clamor grows for universally instituting a civil society, wherein individuals can pursue interests of their own choosing in reciprocity with others, enjoying equal economic opportunity under conditions of a publicly regulated market. Finally, at the summit of politics, constitutional democracy continues to widen its authority even as it grapples with the problem of preventing privileged social interests from subverting political freedom.

Yet on the other hand, just as the institutions of freedom become more and more the universal goal of practice, the very legitimacy of freedom has come under a growing and insidious challenge. This challenge resides not so much in the backwater efforts of ethnic nationalists and religious fundamentalists to unify the remnants of collapsing empires under principles extraneous to self-determination. The more insidious challenge finds its greatest voice in the heart of the oldest democracies and civil societies, where, under the multiple banners of post-modernism, the very autonomy of reason and conduct has come under suspicion. The ever more fashionable view is that the long-prized autonomy of thinking and action is a delusion, quaintly obscuring how all reasoning and conduct is irreducibly caught within given frameworks that impose standards of truth and right relative to historical epoch and cultural milieu, as well as to particular standpoints within each historical-linguistic community rooted in class, gender, race, sexual orientation, and the like. Far from being able to escape the hold of givenness and question reigning authority in theory and practice, reason and conduct are ineluctably foundation-ridden, condemned to lay claim to values that always issue from privileged terms that cannot be questioned precisely because all attempts at justification can proceed only upon their basis or that of some other arbitrarily given paradigms.

In this way, the problem of foundationalism, so roundly denounced as a dilemma sabotaging the traditional aspirations of theoretical and practical philosophy, has now been wearily accepted as a fate from which there is no escape. The divide between foundationalists and antifoundationalists has turned out to be no divide at all. For the self-proclaimed antifoundationalists have simply abandoned challenging the hold of foundations upon reason and conduct, resigning themselves instead to observing the conversations of mankind, deconstructing philosophy with an edifying metareflection and metaethics, becoming self-conscious of the conceptual schemes that underlie all normative discourse, and at best engaging in a reflective equilibrium that points out how given views might be adjusted to conform more consistently with the given foundations they rest upon.

Many a latter-day antifoundationalist would like to claim that such sober resignation is the only appropriate basis for a liberal society devoted to enabling all its members to pursue their vision of the good on an equal footing. Yet it is hard to see how the embrace of edification fits any less the new aristocracy of the *Übermensch* who openly imposes perspectival particular aims upon all others in a consistent exercise of value positing, which, after all, can be little else but a will to power if all values are arbitrary stipulations.

Is the yawning discrepancy between current theory and practice, between the post-modernist denial of autonomous reason and conduct and the pervasive march toward institutions of freedom, a harbinger of a counterrevolutionary upheaval, overturning the fundamental drift of modernity, or might it signify instead a theoretical blindness to an alternative philosophical strategy that overcomes foundationalism without abandoning the autonomy of reason and action?

Resolving this question requires reconsidering how foundations pose a problem for theory and practice that is neither fortuitous nor unavoidable. Although the endeavor of moving from opinion to knowledge is not entirely akin to that of moving from given convention to valid conduct, each involves parallel challenges of justification, eliciting common strategies in response. These approaches fall into three fundamental types, two of which encompass the entire foundationalist/ antifoundationalist spectrum of current fashion, and one of which remains the ignored odd man out, whose character and validity can best be understood by following out the breakdown of its two more familiar competitors. As it turns out, the status of freedom in theory and practice is determined by the very outcome of exploring each of these strategies in succession, first in the field of theoretical philosophy and then in the field of ethics.[2]

The Appeal to Privileged Givens in Theoretical Philosophy

Whether in regard to thinking thinking or to thinking what is other to thought, philosophy has traditionally found it natural to base the validity of its claims in a privileged given, providing the foundation of ultimate justification for the conception of valid reasoning or of true reality. Any other option has appeared hopeless. For if the uncertainty, the particularity, the subjectivity, the conventionality, and the otherwise conditioned character of belief is to be overcome, how else can it be accomplished other than by discovering a given content that is immediate and thereby dependent on nothing else, that is unconditioned and thereby free of any relativizing factors, that is universal and not limited by particular circumstance, and that is in all these respects presuppositionless. Insofar as truth appears to require presuppositionlessness, universal validity, and self-grounding, what else could command such authority other than a given content that is what it is by nature, rather than as a product or construct of some other factor? Moreover, such a content must not only be immediate, but it must serve as a first principle, providing a self-evident, self-grounded foundation from which all other truths are determined. If other contents cannot be shown to be grounded in such a privileged given, how can they possibly rise above the uncertainty of opinion and share the objectivity and unconditioned universality that such a first principle can alone command?

This consideration applies as much to logic as to conceiving reality. If reason cannot be shown to rest upon one or more self-evident principles from which all other logical moves are derived, how can reasoning claim to have any validity? Analogously, if reality cannot be shown to rest upon a fundamental structure presupposing no other, a structure given immediately to a passive contemplation of what is, how can philosophy pretend to offer a theory of reality unmarred by a reliance upon unsubstantiated factors that are simply taken for granted?

Such are the considerations that have led what has been alternately labeled metaphysical, dogmatic, or precritical philosophy to appeal to privileged givens as the foundation of truth. Whether these privileged terms comprise first principles of reasoning or first principles of reality, they represent contents that are understood to be immediately given by nature rather than by convention and thereby to be presuppositionless, unconditioned, universal, and self-grounding. As such, they are apprehended by a contemplation that passively receives them rather than constructs them, doing so not in virtue of any demonstration, but rather by direct intuition. Accordingly, this metaphysical approach characteristically begins its inquiry by asking what is and directly discovering the fundamental nature of things.

However, whether this investigation takes the form of an ontology of being as such, or an ontotheology of the highest being on which all else depends, or regional ontologies of different spheres of existence, it will face a dilemma that equally afflicts any effort to establish the first principles of reason. If fundamental normativity resides in a privileged given, how can any content be certified to qualify as the sought-after foundation? What can possibly decide which given content commands exclusive authority as that presuppositionless, unconditioned, universally valid term upon which all justification is rooted? Clearly, to search for mediating reasons would be self-defeating, for if the putative foundation owes its privileged role to something else, it forfeits its own constitutive primacy.

Can the first principle then be identified regressively by certifying that all else, whether logical reasonings or all other beings, rests upon it? Yet how, without reliance upon the foundation of justification, can one certify that everything else rests upon any given content? On what basis can one determine the totality of reason or being, or for that matter, what constitutes a proper derivation of that plenitude from the putative foundation?

Appeal to an indirect proof is of little avail. Showing how all known given alternatives collapse through their own incoherence can hardly certify the absence of other unknown options. Moreover, even if one somehow could rule out every other alternative, the remaining candidate still would not be legitimated unless one appealed to a further principle, such as a law of excluded middle, whose own justification would not only remain in question but whose supporting role would once again undermine the alleged primacy of the term it legitimates. Even if, following Aristotle in his argument for the principle of contradiction, one might show that no determinate opposing view could be advanced without endorsing the vaunted candidate, this demonstration would still rest upon prior assumptions about the conditions for something to be or be meant.

The Foundational Dilemmas of Teleological Ethics

Completely parallel difficulties apply in ethics when the justification of conduct is sought in privileged givens. This ploy is the basic strategy defining teleological ethics, which follows the all too plausible path of distinguishing between valid and invalid conduct according to whether it embodies the antecedently determined form of the good.

The rationale for measuring conduct by the good simply translates into another idiom the same line of reasoning that leads metaphysical philosophy to seek foundations for reality and reason. Since all conduct, being voluntary, aims at an end, how else can action be evaluated other than by determining a privileged goal that not only has inherent worth but that provides the rationale for the pursuit of all other ends? Only such a sovereign end-in-itself can provide an unequivocal standard for conduct that does not fall into either the infinite regress of instrumental action, for which no aim can be found whose value does not lie in serving as a means to something else, or the insoluble quandary of choosing among a plurality of ends-in-themselves. To avoid condemning action to an endless pursuit for some reason to choose one goal rather than another, one must discover a highest good, whose validity lies nowhere else but in its own content, which, drawing its validity from no other source but its own immediate givenness, occupies the privileged role of first principle of conduct. Accordingly, ethics can be nothing other than a science of the highest good, which, given its sovereign character as the subordinating end of all other pursuits, is ultimately a form of political life. Conduct will therefore be valid not by exercising its own autonomy in determining its ends but by embodying the given content that reason prescribes for this self-sufficient, unconditioned rule of living. By the same token, law will have authority not in virtue of either who promulgates it or according to what procedure it is enacted but rather in the degree to which its content embodies what the highest good prescribes to be right by nature.

Yet just as first principles of reason and reality are ready victims of skeptical challenge, so the highest good eludes any satisfactory determination. Defined simply as the sovereign end-in-itself to which all other pursuits are subordinated, the highest good is nothing but the formal scaffold of any prevailing political rule that succeeds in lording over all activity, reducing ethics to a nihilism of might makes right. This formality cannot be overcome by appealing to human nature and trying to discover a given function whose best fulfillment might give content to the highest good. Not only can the identity of a human function be questioned, but so can its prescriptive status. For if it is simply a fact of species being, how can it possibly have any independent normative significance? Even to characterize the privileged human function as a matter of acting in accord with reason remains an utterly empty injunction, since all it does is place us once more before the problem of ethics, namely, of determining what indeed it is to act in a rationally justified manner. Further appeal to any other content that is alleged to be what exists by nature meets similar difficulties. Not only can its "natural" givenness be doubted, but so can the very appropriateness of elevating one fact of existence above all others and treating it as an immediately prescriptive rule.

The basic problem is that any attempt to legitimate a particular content as that of the highest good will require appeal to other factors. If these themselves are normative grounds, they undermine the supreme primacy of the highest good, whereas if they are devoid of normative significance, they cannot play any legitimate role in specifying what is of paramount intrinsic worth. Moreover, although the highest good, as that end-in-itself to which all other activity is subordinated, comprises a ruling activity that is for its own sake, it still serves as an antecedent form that conduct needs to embody in order to be valid. Yet how can conduct both embody something determined prior and apart from itself and be action for its own sake? Further, if the mere existence of a mode of conduct cannot supply it with normative validity and no given content can unequivocally qualify itself as the highest good, how can any goal be certified as a valid measure of conduct without appealing to the manner of its selection?

The Appeal to a Privileged Determiner

In theory or practice, the metaphysical strategy of rooting ultimate justification in a privileged given ends up revealing that the only reason for one content rather than another serving a foundational role is that such a position has been conferred upon it by the theorist. No matter how formulated, the foundation is presented by a direct reference to what is that perennially takes for granted the adequacy of the cognition claiming primacy for its reputed givenness. Consequently, the failure of the appeal to privileged givens naturally shifts attention to the positing responsible for producing the putative foundation. Instead of relying upon a passive contemplation making direct reference to what is by nature, ultimate justification must be sought elsewhere—and where else but in that determiner capable of determining what counts as true and objective, not by offering privileged contents but by engaging in a privileged act specifying the very domain of normative validity?

In this way, philosophy has made its transcendental turn away from any dogmatic direct reference to reality, choosing instead an indirect route that supplants the appeal to privileged givens with an appeal to a privileged determiner. In theoretical philosophy, this move entails a foundational epistemology that mandates as the first task of philosophy uncovering the structure of knowing or reference responsible for constructing what counts as true.

The embrace of a foundational epistemology as a preliminary for making possible objective knowledge might appear paradoxical at first glance. Since any direct reference to things in themselves must be ruled out, how can the turn to investigate knowing in its own right possibly establish the objectivity of knowing's claims? The very standard for adjudicating between competing beliefs seems to be wanting, for if all that can be legitimately considered is knowing, and if the truth of knowledge resides in correspondence to its object, how can that correspondence ever be certified by an investigation that restricts its gaze to cognitive structure?

Although the transcendental turn offers itself as the necessary preliminary to a valid conception of reality, the only way it can serve that role is if its conception of knowing ceases to be such a preliminary and instead contains within itself the determination of the object of knowledge to the extent that it can be known with more than pragmatic assurances.[3] For only if objectivity is determined by the structure of knowing can an investigation of knowing apart from reference to objects in themselves possibly bear upon the objectivity of knowledge.[4]

In this way, the transcendental investigation of knowing skirts the dilemma of the representational model of knowing. That model renders knowledge unattainable by construing knowing and its object as given independently from one another, precluding any direct comparison of knowing's representations and their referent. When, by contrast, the object of knowing is taken to be a construct of knowing, an investigation of cognition can lay hold of what is knowable, since objectivity is precisely what knowing puts into its own representations. These representations achieve objective reference not through any comparison with things-in-themselves but rather through relations among representations that can be shown to be necessary to the very structure of cognition and, in that sense, intersubjectively valid rather than merely subjectively at hand.

Consequently, the transcendental turn does not simply alter the order of philosophical investigation by putting epistemology first, in place of ontology. Rather, transcendental philosophy equally transforms objectivity into a construct of the structure of cognition. What counts as valid is therefore no longer immediately given but rather mediated by a structure of reference that is to be certified as the privileged epistemological foundation from which and for which objectivity is determined.

It is therefore no accident that objectivity is construed by Kant, the great pioneer of the appeal to privileged determiners, as a domain of nature governed by the necessity of efficient causality. Since objectivity can now be legitimately known only insofar as it is determined from without by the structure of knowing, objectivity will be ordered by an external necessity. Moreover, since what is universal and necessary in objectivity issues from the unitary structure of knowing, which applies equally to all possible objects of knowledge, objectivity will have to be a nature governed by laws that apply to objects in general, irrespective of what kind of thing they are. If objects are to be known as enduring substances, they therefore will not be modeled after artifacts, combining an intelligible form imposed upon an indeterminate matter, but rather as entities whose lawfulness pertains to their homogeneous sensuous materiality, enabling them to be known by means of an empirical science.

This limitation poses notorious problems for the Kantian version of transcendental philosophy, for it excludes from the domain of objectivity living organisms, objects of beauty, and, above all, rational agents, none of which are intelligible solely in terms of efficient causality. With living selves unable to appear to themselves or to one another as such within the field of objectivity, self-consciousness, so central to the Kantian conception of cognition, becomes just as unfathomable as moral relations, which involve the mutual recognizability of persons.

These problems, together with Kant's equally notorious reference to things-in-themselves and his metaphysical deduction of the categories, might appear to be remedial failings of a first trailblazer rather than fatal difficulties endemic to transcendental philosophy in general. And indeed subsequent philosophy has been largely occupied with saving the transcendental project from the acknowledged blunders that Kant committed in pioneering its strategy.

Starting with Fichte and continuing with Husserl, latter-day transcendental philosophers have recognized that Kant's residual reference to things-in-themselves involves just as much a retreat to a dogmatic appeal to the given as does Kant's appropriation of the table of categories from the forms of judgment of traditional logic. To remedy these inadvertent lapses, Fichte and Husserl have tried to eliminate any transcendent domain beyond the limits of transcendental constitution and to extend transcendental constitution beyond empirical objects to include the categories and forms of judgment themselves. After all, if validity cannot reside in privileged givens, then no knowledge claims of any sort can legitimately be made that cannot be referred back to the structure of cognition.

For similar reasons, thinkers from Schelling to Heidegger and Wittgenstein have attempted to remove the divide between the domain of objectivity and the transcendental structures themselves. Noumenal subjectivity has been replaced by such "objectified" conditions of knowing as the interest-laden being-in-the-world of *Dasein* and the intersubjective structures of linguistic reference and cultural interpretation. Unless the conditions of knowing can be removed from the noumenal realm and brought down to earth in the form of such tangible practices as language games, how can the transcendental structures be known with any more authority than the objects of knowledge they are reputed to make possible?

Yet can either of these complementary extensions of transcendental argument surmount the difficulties at which they are aimed? If all reference to the given is strictly forbidden, leaving an internal realism wherein objectivity is explicitly the stipulation of knowing, to what degree is solipsism avoidable? Can idealism be refuted without situating knowing in a framework that it has not totally constituted?

Moreover, can all features of the transcendental structure be determined in just the same way in which objects of knowledge are transcendentally constituted? The case of Husserl is instructive. Although Husserl, to his credit, is pointedly aware of the need to avoid any direct reference to the conditions of knowing, he recognizes that the moment an aspect of the transcendental structure is traced back to an act of transcendental constitution, that very act must itself be constituted by a further transcendental reflection if it is not to represent a new given to which dogmatic reference is made. Yet, as Husserl must admit, as long as object and act of knowing, *noema* and *noesis*, are differentiated, as they must be to prevent intentionality from collapsing, transcendental investigation can *never* account for all its terms. Whenever an act of knowing is shown to constitute a type of object, that act stands in need of a further act to account for its own determination for knowing. Phenomenological investigation must thus remain an infinite striving, whose incompleteness testifies to an ineradicable element of givenness in the transcendental structure itself.

This residue of givenness in transcendental investigation should come as no surprise. The moment that foundational epistemology supplants ontology as first philosophy, the transcendental investigator cannot help but make direct appeal to a certain structure as the condition of valid knowing. That the chosen structure is adequately described and that it have the exclusive privilege of determining objectivity are matters that cannot be established *after* the transcendental investigation has purportedly legitimated the scope and authority of knowledge, for the character of the conditions of knowing are, as such, the prior determinants of true knowledge, from which knowledge of particular objects can first be gained. It does not matter whether the transcendental conditions are described as noumenal subjectivity, linguistic practice, hermeneutic reflection, relations of production, or in any other terms. In every case, they occupy their privileged role as the constituting structure of objectivity insofar as their character and status are antecedent to the knowledge they make possible. For this reason, transcendental conditions can only be referred to in the same way as dogmatic philosophy made direct reference to its privileged givens. For although the investigation of the conditions of knowing is intended as a necessary preliminary to any knowledge of particular objects, it itself engages in a knowing of a subject matter of its own, exercising what Hegel would castigate as a "knowing before knowing."

Transforming the transcendental conditions into tangible practices having the same character as the objectivity they constitute cannot obviate the anomaly. Such a "naturalization" of epistemology only introduces the confusion of what Husserl branded as "psychologism," where the putative conditions of knowing are described in terms of the very objectivity that must first be accounted for as something determined by the structure of knowing. When, for instance, a Quine analyzes the limits of reference in terms of the empirical behavior of speakers, the description of that behavior is immediately given as anything but ontologically relative through a direct reference whose legitimacy is no more questioned than Wittgenstein's own reference to language games.[5]

The underlying problem bedeviling all of these efforts of transcendental philosophy is the abiding discrepancy between the knowing exercised by the transcendental investigator and the knowing under critique. Logically speaking, this discrepancy exhibits the perennial incoherence of any foundationalism: namely, that the privileged factor that confers normativity does not and indeed cannot itself enjoy the validity it provides. In the case of foundational epistemology, where the appeal to a privileged determiner has supplanted the appeal to privileged givens, the discrepancy consists in how objectivity is constituted by the transcendental structures of knowing, whereas these very structures, as prior determiners, have their character antecedent to their own act of constitution. As a consequence, they cannot possess a like objectivity of their own without canceling the distinction between the conditions of knowing and objects of knowledge, a distinction upon which the very possibility of a transcendental investigation rests.

The need to overcome this discrepancy is nevertheless inherent in the transcendental turn, once due attention is paid to the problem of removing any last residue of privileged givenness and the dogmatic reference to which it corresponds. Transcendental inquiry must question the authority of its own transcendental knowledge and certify the validity of its own knowing of the knowing under critique. In order for this transcendental knowledge to be valid, it must have precisely the same character that it discovers to be constitutive of valid knowing. Otherwise its cognition of the conditions of knowing will not conform to the standards of true knowing. Yet for this to be the case, the metareflection of the transcendental philosopher must lose its difference from the knowing it reflects upon, or, in other words, knowing must do its own critique. Since what foundational epistemology knows is what is to be determined to be valid knowing, its own transcendental knowledge consists in a knowing of valid knowing. However, in order for this knowing to conform to what it knows, valid knowing must itself be a knowing of valid knowing. Then, however, the difference between knowing and its object disappears and with it any distinction between the conditions of knowing and what they condition. Transcendental inquiry thereby annuls itself, for knowing can be investigated on its own as a preliminary to obtaining knowledge of objects only if knowing and its object can be differentiated. Or, to put the outcome in purely logical terms, the conferring source of normative validity ceases to be a privileged determiner of something other than itself, thereby shedding its own given character as a prior condition.

The Dilemmas of Liberalism

The significance of this result is most palpable in the complementary form it takes when ethics abandons the search for a highest good and instead shifts the locus of normativity in conduct from the given content of ends and institutions to the source or procedure from which they issue. With the breakdown of teleological ethics exhibiting how no actions or conventions can enjoy validity based upon the content they embody, agents are liberated from any duty to realize any ends alleged to be given by nature or dictated by reason independently of their willing. By itself, this liberation from the external prescription of substantive ends does not confer legitimacy to the liberty of individuals to pursue ends of their own choosing, since the inability to determine a highest good leaves equally open the option of nihilism, for which liberty has no more value than any candidate for the good. Nevertheless, just as the repudiation of the metaphysical search for first principles of reason and reality made it plausible to turn to investigate knowing as a preliminary to comprehending what is, so the denial of a determinable highest good paves the way for an appeal to the most plausible of privileged determiners in the field of practice, the individual will underlying all conduct and institutions. Instead of residing in conformity with the antecedent content of the good, normative validity now consists in being determined by whatever exercise of will is ascribed primacy. In this respect, ethics becomes a procedural theory, where valid practice enjoys authority not because its content conforms to any given standard but because it can be shown to be determined by a privileged method of willing. The latter plays the archimedean role of being bound by no prior norms, but instead automatically conferring legitimacy to whatever issues from it.

This foundational exercise can be interpreted in an empiricist manner, according to which liberty consists in the entitled freedom to act in pursuit of given desires. Due to the repudiation of any prior rational hierarchy of ends or corresponding virtues and character, these desires all stand on just as much a par as each and every will. Consequently, the primacy of the liberty of desire translates into a utilitarian principle by which normative validity lies in any course of action or institutional arrangement that promotes the greatest aggregate satisfaction of the desires of all. Laws and legal procedures will accordingly be valid to the degree that they enhance the general welfare as measured by the utilitarian calculus.

However, the empiricist interpretation of liberty thereby binds the will to a pursuit of given ends, whose contingent facticity makes any utilitarian calculus problematic and reintroduces a domain of privileged givenness. Consequently, procedural ethics is impelled to overcome such heteronomy and interpret its privileged exercise of freedom in an a priori fashion, in which entitled freedom consists in acting independently of given desires according to a rational form of willing whose privileged exercise comprises a principle of right preempting any prior interpretation of the good. Thus, the legal order will be valid not according to how it promotes the general happiness or otherwise commands agents to pursue specific ends but according to how it regulates actions in conformity with respect for the privileged form of willing. Whether this legal regulation emanates from the command of a sovereign empowered by covenant, from the colegislation of a general will, or from a privileged choice procedure operating behind a veil of ignorance, the validity of law resides in how it issues from the proper determiner.

Either way, empirically conditioned or a priori, the liberty that is accorded primacy functions as an antecedent principle of valid conduct and institutions. They are legitimate by being determined by it. Consequently, whether construed as a liberty of desire or as the autonomy of a practical reason, the privileged procedural factor has a given character that precedes what its application determines to be moral and just. As a result, neither itself nor the conduct and institutions that issue from it exhibit self-determination proper. The practice that owes its normativity to issuing from a privileged procedure is determined by that prior procedure, which, in determining that derivative domain, does not give itself any further character, but rather specifies something other than itself. Logically speaking, the freedom embraced by these varieties of liberalism exhibits the two-tiered structure of a logic of essence, where one term posits another. By contrast, in self-determination, what does the determining is one and the same as what is determined. When the will is treated as a principle, it is relegated to the status of a prior positor whose character is given antecedently to its act of positing. In other words, just as the transcendental conditions of knowing necessarily possess an element of givenness in their own prior description, so procedural ethics offers a principle of willing whose own character is just as given as any candidate for the highest good.

This residual element of givenness afflicting the appeal to liberty shows its problematic character on two fronts: first, in face of the specter of formalism haunting its efforts to unequivocally derive determinate norms and institutions from its privileged procedure, second, and most crucially, when the very authority of the proffered principle of willing is called into question.

Formalism enters in because the privileged procedure comprises a mode of willing whose character is given prior to its own exercise. Accordingly, it constitutes a capacity—rather than an actuality—which must draw the content of its actual exercise from some other source. Thus, the privileged liberty of utilitarianism draws its ends from empirical desire, whereas the formal willing of Kantian autonomy must still rely upon the given content of maxims to supply it with anything to test for universalizability. Under these conditions, how can the determining of the privileged procedure really signify a departure from the teleological reliance upon privileged givens? In order to determine whether a course of action conforms to the formal principle, must not some additional criteria of application be introduced, undermining the exclusive normativity of the procedure? In this vein, for instance, Hegel points out that Kant's disqualification of borrowing funds with no intention of repayment as nonuniversalizable illicitly presupposes a commitment to property.

Habermas's communicative ethics brings this dilemma to perhaps its most absurd and telling form when he proudly admits that his ideal speech situation of nondistorted communication is such that one cannot predict, prior to its exercise, what norms and institutions will be agreed upon as sanctioned practices. Yet since his privileged speech situation is not an actual normative institution, but an ideal procedure for determining what is just, there can never be any opportunity to observe what might issue from its operation. Hence, communicative ethics collapses into sheer indeterminacy, effacing itself as an alternative to the teleological option against which it rebels.

Even more threatening, however, is the dilemma inescapably surrounding the legitimacy of the privileged procedure, given its own repudiation of rooting normativity in any given end or institution.

Whereas the privileged procedure should not be bound by any independently given norms, everything of normative standing should issue from its application. Yet how then can its own content be justified? Does not, for instance, Rawls's description of the original position or Habermas's characterization of the ideal speech situation rest upon a prior commitment to liberty and a corresponding impartial respect for individual interests, which, as such, cannot issue from the procedure it grounds? Or more generally, must not any privileged procedure owe its own determination to a source given independently of its own application, thereby undercutting the archimedean role it otherwise claims for itself? This is the very same problem that afflicts the givenness of the transcendental conditions, whose own character cannot possess the certified objectivity they themselves reputedly constitute.

Little relief is obtained by openly admitting the foundational character of the privileged procedure, as Rawls effectively does in acknowledging that the original position merely conforms to our given moral intuitions and thus can only frame *a*, rather than *the*, theory of justice, bringing a degree of consistency to the historically relative ethics of our community. This admission can only bear upon the fate of ethics if a supplementary argument shows that no other alternatives are possible. Yet can such an argument be delivered by a thinking resigned to the foundation-ridden relativism of reflective equilibrium?

As in the case of foundational epistemology, the dilemma demanding a solution lies in the abiding discrepancy between what possesses normativity and what confers normativity. The true can no more be determined by what lacks truth than right can be determined by what stands outside the domain of valid conduct. In each case, the problem of foundationalism points towards eliminating the divide between foundation and what is founded, between procedure and derivative norms; yet canceling the divide is precisely what eliminates the very enterprise of these respective theoretical strategies.

The collapse of procedural ethics thus confirms how in practical as well as in theoretical philosophy the appeal to privileged determiners fares no better than the appeal to privileged givens. With the demise of these complementary foundationalisms, normative validity may be freed from the dilemmas of conformity with any privileged givens or determination by any privileged determiner. Does this liberation, however, signify an end to philosophy, where the collapse of the dual foundationalisms of foundational ontology and teleological ethics, on the one hand, and foundational epistemology and liberalism, on the other, leave no other option in their wake? These two brands of foundationalism may well garner the lion's share of philosophical history, but can this fact legitimate the post-modern turn to supplant philosophical investigation with edifying deconstructions of given theories?

The Dogmatism of the Post-Modern Turn

In order for the failure of the two varieties of foundationalism to condemn philosophy to impotence, a valid argument must establish that they exhaust the possibilities of philosophical inquiry. But can the would-be gravediggers of philosophy succeed at their therapeutic game if, to do so, they must make definitive claims about the options of philosophical reason? Can philosophical argument be employed to cure us of philosophy?

Far from overcoming philosophy, post-modernism's turn to edifying deconstruction is, if anything, a regression to the very foundationalism it seeks to avoid. For when the post-modernist depicts the conversation of mankind as foundation-ridden and then proceeds to lay bare the conceptual schemes supposedly underlying various philosophical projects, the post-modernist reverts to dogmatic foundationalism by making direct reference to the foundation-ridden practice of discourse and then treats it as a transcendental condition of knowing, never bothering to reflect on what legitimacy these claims can have in their own right.

If post-modernism denies that it mirrors the reality of discourse or transcendentally constitutes historically contingent paradigms of knowledge and conduct, it fares no better in opting for a holism in which truth and right are seen to reside in coherence with our historically given web of belief and the practices that underlie and sustain it. Once again, the post-modernist must explain how reference can be made to that encompassing web of theory and practice in terms of coherence, since that web itself either cannot be known at all, given the lack of anything further with which it can cohere, or it must be known directly, in flagrant contradiction to the coherence theory itself.[6]

The Normativity of Autonomy in Theory

How then can philosophical investigation possibly proceed in the face of post-modernism's failure to condemn philosophy to foundationalism and foundationalism's own collapse in both its forms? By themselves, the breakdowns of the appeals to privileged givens and privileged determiners in theory and practice offer little more than a negative prescription: the quests for truth and right must free themselves of foundations and somehow operate without making any assumptions concerning either the content of their respective topics or the method of their treatment. With respect to philosophy in general, this rejection of foundations mandates that philosophical investigation must proceed without any preconception of form or content. Indeed, since all questions of the subject matter and method of philosophy are themselves philosophical issues, they must be addressed within philosophy itself rather than accepted as matters settled prior to the exercise of philosophical reason. Escaping the appeal to privileged givens and privileged determiners is thus tantamount to achieving a thoroughly radical presuppositionlessness, not in the bogus way of stipulating specific contents and procedures as if they were beyond assumption, but by beginning with no determinate givens whatsoever. Yet if this negative prescription leaves philosophy with the prospect of beginning with nothing at all, it has a positive significance that is the other side of the negative freedom from foundations.

Whereas philosophy can begin with no determinate claims concerning reality or knowing, any determinate subject matter that arises for philosophical inquiry must be generated wholly within that inquiry and arise in an ordering that itself emerges without reliance upon any externally given principles or procedures. In this respect, a philosophy free of foundations is, in the first instance, a theory of determinacy as such. Neither metaphysical nor transcendental inquiry can provide such a theory precisely because any such foundationalisms proceed from given determinacies of one sort or another, precluding any account of determinacy in general. Only an investigation that begins without any determinate foundations, without any determinate claims about what is or about knowing, can possibly account for this most minimal of contents, whose lack of treatment testifies to the dogmatism of any other approach.[7] Yet if philosophy can be and in fact cannot help but be a theory of determinacy by starting without foundations, its account of determinacy is no less an account of self-determined determinacy, that is, of self-determination per se.

Philosophy without foundations turns out to present self-determined determinacy because, given the exclusion of any external factors, whatever content and ordering it can possibly achieve will have to be self-generated. Starting with indeterminacy, philosophical investigation can only consist in a self-developing conceptual process, whose subject matter orders itself. Since this self-development proceeds from no given substrate or determining standpoint, it will not comprise the self-determination of any given content, but rather will be self-determination per se.

This outcome does not signal the embrace of a new foundation, where self-determination supplants given determinacy and determined determinacy as the ground of normativity. Precisely because self-determination is what it is as a result of its own determination, it can have no given content. For this reason, self-determination must proceed from indeterminacy, and any attempt to treat self-determination as a principle automatically falsifies it, transforming it into a privileged determiner whose own content is given rather than self-informed.

By issuing in the self-exposition of self-determination as the positive side of the liberation from foundations, philosophy is able to attain the self-grounding, unconditioned universality and presuppositionlessness that has always eluded philosophical reason as long as it appealed to privileged contents and privileged standpoints. Self-determination is the very logic of self-grounding precisely because it owes its character to nothing but itself. By the same token, self-determination enjoys unconditioned universality insofar as what it is is independent of any condition or particular factor. Finally, self-determination is the positive outcome of presuppositionlessness precisely because it alone provides a content that rests on no prior terms.

In all these converging respects, self-determination turns out to be the very logic of normativity. The truth of the categories comprising its self-development lies neither in correspondence to any independent givens, nor in coherence with any antecedent totality, nor in being constituted by any privileged conditions of reference. It instead lies in the very freedom from extraneous determination, which, positively expressed, could be called categorial immanence. That is, the truth of the categories of a foundation-free philosophy will reside in how they arise from one another in an order dependent on nothing but their own content, proceeding from indeterminacy. Since self-determined determinacy comes to be what it is only as the outcome of its process, what its constitutive categories are categories of is only determinable as the result of the process. By the same token, the ordering principle or method of their development will also only emerge at the very end, for the ordering unity of the development is nothing other than self-determination itself. Consequently, completely contrary to foundationalism, the subject matter and method of philosophy will not be given at the outset but will be arrived at as the outcome of philosophical investigation. In this way, philosophy will exhibit a radically autonomous reason, whose negative and positive freedom from any external determination is the very mark of its normative validity.

Philosophy will thereby be systematic to the very degree that it is antifoundationalist. Whereas foundational theories root the introduction and ordering of their content on arbitrary givens, philosophy without foundations will have to present the self-development of its subject matter, whose own resultant determination will confirm precisely the order in which it must present itself. At each stage, no term can be legitimately introduced that involves more than those that are already at hand. Yet, because the whole process proceeds from indeterminacy rather than from first principles, each prior term will have to give rise to what is other than itself as the outcome of its very own determination. In this way, each move will operate as a determinate negation, where the only resource providing for the introduction of new content will be the preceding categories, whose own specification will involve their own supersession and passage into a term incorporating them without being reducible to them. Accordingly, at every point along the way, what gets treated will be just as nonarbitrary as when it comes into view. Although this strict systematicity stands so opposed to the familiar paths of metaphysical reference and transcendental constitution, it is nothing more than the fulfillment of the perennial demand of philosophical self-responsibility: that contents not be introduced until after all their prerequisites have been established.

This identification of freedom from foundations with systematicity, whereby philosophy achieves presuppositionlessness by proceeding as a theory of determinacy presenting the self-exposition of self-determination, can further be identified as the science of logic.[8] As the prescriptive discipline that seeks to think validly what is valid thinking, logic can hardly achieve its constitutive aim if it allows any aspect of its method or content to be preconceived. Whereas other disciplines have a subject matter distinct from the method by which it is examined, prescriptive logic investigates precisely what it must employ to capture its prey. To be the valid thinking of valid thinking, prescriptive logic's form and content must be one. For this very reason, logic cannot begin with any preestablished method without utterly begging the question. By the same token, logic cannot begin with any determinate subject matter, since what valid thinking is is precisely what its own investigation must establish. Consequently, prescriptive logic must begin without any foundations and end up presenting the self-thinking of valid thought, which, as such, cannot help but be a wholly autonomous development. Since its autonomy proceeds from no antecedent content or method, prescriptive logic ends up being the same theory of self-determination per se that philosophy begins with once it frees itself from foundations.[9]

These brief anticipations of how reason attains normative validity by achieving a foundation-free autonomy are so contrary to prevailing fashion that they have an almost unintelligible ring, despite the detailed efforts long made to bring them to fruition, above all by Hegel in his much-neglected *Science of Logic*. The normativity of autonomous reason, however, has a tangible corroboration in the completely analogous overcoming of foundations in ethics and in modernity's parallel struggle to replace tradition with institutions of freedom in every sphere of conduct.

The Normativity of Autonomy in Practice

Although liberalism already brings freedom to center stage in ethics, it commits the foundationalist blunder of treating self-determination as a first principle, transforming it into a liberty defined by nature, by the self, or by some other factor prior to the practices and institutions that are ascribed legitimacy by being determined by its antecedent form. As the dilemmas of procedural ethics make most patent, normativity in conduct cannot be coherently determined unless what confers normativity no longer stands apart from what possesses normative validity. In order for conduct to escape the insoluble dilemmas of foundationalism, valid conduct and institutions must thus be determined by nothing other than themselves. That is, normative validity in conduct can be none other than the reality of self-determination.

However, if freedom is not to revert to a determining principle of derivative institutions, self-determination can no longer be conceived apart from legitimate institutions. Instead, self-determination must itself comprise a system of institutions of freedom exhausting normativity in practice. Accordingly, freedom will no longer be determined as a function of the self, given independently of the interactions of agents. Instead, freedom will consist of autonomous interrelations of individuals, which, given their identity with normative practice, will comprise objectively recognized entitled exercises of freedom. These interrelations will thereby consist in practices in which agents exercise specific rights, which, as entitlements of each and every participating agent, will be exercised in conjunction with observing the correlative duty of respecting the same right of those with whom one interrelates. Accordingly, freedom, at one with justice, will consist in structures of reciprocal recognition, in which agents interrelate by determining themselves in conformity with honoring the correlative self-determination of their counterparts.

If the connection between the different structures of right is not to rest upon a given foundation undermining their autonomy, the unity of this system must itself be the product of one of its own constitutive modes of self-determination. Only then can agency be genuinely self-determined, for only within a self-ordered system of enacted modes of freedom can agents engage in action where they determine both the form and content of their agency. As long as agency is confined to the isolated deeds of the single self, it cannot avoid being defined in terms of the logic of positing, as a determiner whose own structure precedes what it determines. Admittedly, one cannot do without the corresponding "natural" will of the individual, since no institutions can function without each of their participants employing a will whose faculty of choice is given prior to any decision they take. Nevertheless, this faculty of choice no more determines which of the actions it can select count as valid practice than conditions of discourse, whether language, consciousness, or, for that matter, digestion, can determine which of the claims they make possible is true. Only within the enacted contexts of a system of rights, such as comprise property relations, a moral community, a free family, a civil society, and a constitutional democracy, can individuals achieve genuine self-determination, determining both who they are and what they will in their "artificial" capacities as autonomous owners, moral subjects, family members, economic agents, and citizens. In so doing, they exercise objectively recognized modes of autonomy that cannot be performed apart from the interactions to which they belong, interactions which themselves consist in nothing but the respected exercise of the freedoms they make possible. Moreover, to the extent that one of these structures of interaction involves a political freedom of constitutional self-government that unifies the entire system of freedoms into a self-ordered whole, containing its standard within itself, individuals are able to engage in a self-determination that thoroughly grounds all dimensions of their autonomy. In this way, autonomous conduct animates a conventional world of its own whose normative character is determined independently of any given foundations.

Accordingly, just as philosophy in general overcomes foundations by systematically developing autonomous reason, ethics surmounts the challenge of post-modernism by conceiving the self-ordered system of the institutions of freedom. Insofar as this system consists in the respected reality of self-determination, justice is not a matter of embodying a highest good or being the outcome of the proper choice procedure or cohering with any historically given community. Valid practice instead consists in nothing but the concordant exercise of rights in all their different spheres. Therefore, what gives modernity its abiding standard can be none other than the philosophy of right, whose conception of self-determination prescribes what ought to be done.

Hence, in theory or practice, to ignore the normativity of autonomy is to live on one's knees. In the case of the philosophy of law, freedom from foundations liberates legal thought from the dogmatic formalism of value-neutral inquiry and sets the investigation of law squarely within the philosophy of right. Conceiving law in this context is the challenge to which autonomous reason must now freely turn.

2 · The System of Right as the Frame of Law

Law in Context

With reason overcoming the dilemmas of foundationalism by identifying self-determination and normativity, the common bases of legal positivism and communitarian conventionalism are overturned. The institutions of conduct are no longer beyond rational justification, giving license to a value-neutral, formal treatment of ethics and law. Meta-ethics and formal legal theory have lost their own rationale, for now conceiving the divide between the ethical and the nonethical cannot leave undetermined the differentiation between the ethical and the unethical, the moral and the immoral, or the just and the unjust. Now that normativity has been found to reside in self-determination, the domain of normative conduct is nothing other than the reality of the institutions of freedom, leaving the unethical immediately identifiable as each and every violation of right, that is, any oppression, any obstruction of the exercise of entitled freedom.

Since law can hardly lie outside the reality of freedom, legal theory cannot address its subject matter as a world apart, indifferent to the different spheres of right. Instead, law must be conceived in context, taking full account of the various institutions of freedom and of how law figures within them.

Yet how is this context to be determined? What signal features differentiate the spheres of right and determine their relation to one another? The normativity of self-determination mandates that the reality of freedom and the institutions of right be one. For this unity to be the case, freedom cannot be a capacity given by nature or a function of the self. It must rather consist in the entire system of the institutions of valid conduct. To the degree that there is more than one mode of freedom, this system will involve a plurality of structures of interaction, each of which comprises an exercise of right with its own medium and corresponding type of agency. In every such interaction, individuals will all engage in a specific form of self-determination, whose realization is predicated upon respecting and being respected by others in their own complementary exercise of that freedom. Only through such reciprocal recognition, where the exercise of right involves honoring the duty to respect the same right of others, can individuals individuate themselves and determine their relation to one another in function of their freedom. This achievement is what makes the connection between self-determination and the mutuality of right and duty indissoluble. Whatever the specific content of any structure of right, it will comprise an interaction in which agents exercise a form of agency that is determined by its own willing. For, unlike the capacity of choice, which is given prior to any decision, the exercise of an entitled freedom can only proceed within a non-natural, artificial structure of mutual recognition whose own existence is defined by nothing other than the acts of will that figure within it. Since rights are not privileges, but universal entitlements, an agent enjoys the exercise of a right only in conjunction with being obliged to honor others' entitlement to do the same. Hence, an agent has a right only in the framework of mutual recognition in which individuals determine themselves in function of respecting each others' autonomy. As a consequence, their acts determine not only an objectification of the will that is mediated by the willing of others, but the very form of agency that is thereby exercised together with the relation between agents in terms of which they are individuated. On all three accounts, which supply respectively the particular, universal and individual dimensions of autonomy, individuals are able to achieve self-determination, willing both a content specific to willing and individuating their own agency through the acts they engage in. Moreover, the freedom they thereby enjoy has an objective actuality residing in the intersubjective conjunction of right and duty constitutive of its exercise.

The mere concept of such normative freedom, which overcomes foundations by realizing the logic of self-determination rather than remaining caught in the logic of positing, may be an ingredient of every right. Nevertheless, it directly entails two particular modes of self-determination circumscribing the system of justice.

The first such mode is directly at hand if the concept of self-determination is taken without further qualification, as simply a structure of interaction in which agents achieve an objectively recognized domain for their freedom, mediated by no further factors or considerations. This minimal specification of self-determination comprises a sphere of property rights, where agents individuate themselves as owners by giving their wills a recognizable reality in an external factor.

If all dimensions of willing are to be self-determined, however, then the connection of any plurality of institutions of freedom will have to be made from within, by a particular mode of autonomy that unifies the whole system of right in the exercise of its own characteristic freedom. If, instead, the unity of the spheres of right lay outside them all in practices or other factors given independently of self-determination, freedom would have its own order imposed upon it by an external foundation, robbing it of any true independence and depriving conduct of normative validity. Consequently, whereas property relations may comprise the minimal reality of freedom, that reality must contain an autonomy ordering the whole of right, exercising a self-rule that enables the reality of freedom to rest upon its own exercise. This, of course, comprises an exercise of political freedom, whose self-government upholds all the other spheres of right in conformity with its own self-rule.

What are the basic features of these extremities of the system of freedom, and how can their poles be bridged to specify the other spheres of right, giving law its normative frame?[1]

The Primacy of Property

If one were to ask, With what must ethics begin? the answer would be nothing other than, "with property rights." Property relations provide the starting point of ethics on two complementary counts, reflecting the overcoming of foundations in conduct.

On the one hand, property comes first to the degree that self-determination is the substance of normativity in practice and the minimal determination of freedom is the interaction in which agents determine themselves as having a recognized reality embodying the autonomy of their respective wills.

On the other hand, the primacy of the right of property in the order of conception and of the reality of freedom implies that all further structures of self-determination presuppose and incorporate the self-determination of owners. For, in order to avoid appeals to arbitrary givens or arbitrary procedures, the philosophy of right must address the reality of freedom by starting with its most minimal specification and advance to more determinate modes of self-determination only after their prerequisite components have already been established.

Yet does the right of ownership have this dual character as the starting point of the conception of freedom? The conceptual primacy of property has, of course, been challenged by Marxists, who would ground property rights in commodity relations; by teleological theorists, who would ground the legitimacy of ownership in its contribution to the realization of the good; and by certain liberal theorists, who would ground the right to property in prior entitlements of distributive justice. All of these challenges are undermined by the foundational commitments underlying their normative claims: by philosophical anthropology in the case of Marxism, by the appeal to the good in teleological ethics, and by the appeal to privileged determiners in liberal theory. Yet even if their objections are freed of such groundings and simply considered as claims that other structures of right underlie property relations, their fate is no better. All of these challenges are demolished either by showing that the concept of self-determination without further qualification is the interaction of property ownership or by showing how all further relations of right necessarily presuppose property rights.

The latter refutation might appear to be the most cumbersome, since it seems to require developing the entire philosophy of right. Yet the fact that all other relations of freedom presuppose property entitlements can be readily seen without entering into an analysis of their specific interactions. The reason why no agent can enjoy any right without already being recognized as a property owner is that, stripped of the right of ownership, an individual is no longer a person with a respected objective domain of self-determination, free from domination by the will of another, but a rightless factor, as susceptible to enslavement as any other entity of potential ownership. Without, in particular, recognized ownership of one's body, an agent can engage in no act in his or her own right, whether in the family, in the market, in the state, or even in the community of morally accountable subjects. This requirement is patently the case in regard to commodity relations, which can hardly generate property entitlements given that commodity exchange can only proceed when the parties to the exchange already have recognized ownership of the goods they bring to market. The same can be said of any imperatives of distributive justice that might be alleged to precede the right to property. After all, if nothing can already count as properly belonging to an agent, how can any distribution set goods and benefits into a rightful relation to persons?[2] Whatever is allotted can no more be the property of the beneficiaries than a bone thrown to a dog can thereby become something to which it is entitled. For if an agent is not already recognized to enjoy self-ownership, that agent is no better than a slave, to whom nothing need be given and from whom anything can be taken if it suits the will of its master. Hence, the right of property is prior to and therefore on its own account indifferent to considerations of distributive justice.

Particular dimensions of ownership may well be subsequently impinged upon by household duties of alimony and child support; by the redistributive imperatives of equal economic opportunity; by the upholding of a legal system through jury duty, public funding and other impositions; and by the exigencies of self-government, which may require persons to risk their life and forfeit some of their property in the defence of democracy. In each case, however, these restrictions of property rights have legitimacy only insofar as they promote the institutions of freedom, which cannot completely obliterate the property rights of persons without subverting their own practices by reducing individuals to slaves, incapable of being free citizens, let alone the holders of any economic, legal, or family rights. Accordingly, recognition of property entitlements, however circumscribed by the requirements of other modes of self-determination, is a structural prerequisite of every institution of freedom, without which their own constitutive roles and activities collapse.

This fundamental ordering has been fatally ignored by contractarians from Hobbes to Rawls and Habermas. Hobbes, though admitting that property is a precondition of justice, still conceives the civil rights of the members of a commonwealth without first accounting for their status as owners;[3] Rawls and Habermas define their privileged procedures for choosing the principles of justice without an antecedent

account of property entitlements. Such contractarian theorists overlook how individuals deprived of recognition as owners lack the respected autonomy either to enter into a covenant or to participate in
an original position or ideal speech situation in which everyone's self-
selected interest is accorded equal weight.

Owing to property right's indispensability for all other modes of self-
determination, being an owner is the necessary and sufficient condition for being a person, that is, for being entitled to right in general.
Although enjoying the physical and mental endowments of rational
agency might qualify one as a *potential* person, one cannot exercise any
further freedoms and achieve the *actuality* of self-determined agency
unless one is accorded the standing of an owner of property. Accordingly, it is more appropriate to follow Hegel and use the term "person"
interchangeably with "property owner" than to follow Kant and conflate personhood with moral subjectivity, whose more determinate,
inwardly reflected mode of agency itself presupposes and incorporates
the status of property owner.[4] For even if morality focuses upon the
purposes, intentions, and conscience of agents, their morally accountable actions must count as their own, rather than as responsibilities of
a master to whom they could otherwise belong.

Property Rights without Legality

What then, are the elementary, nonderivative dimensions of self-
determination that property rights provide as the first stage in the
frame of law? Property comprises the most abstract right of all insofar
as it involves the minimal self-determination of agents by means of the
most immediate of factors. Exercising the entitlement of ownership is
the most elementary of rights because it consists in no more than an
agent giving its freedom some determinate external reality that is
recognized to be the embodiment of that agent's will by other agents
who concordantly determine themselves in precisely the same manner. By participating in this most minimal reciprocal interaction, one
determines oneself simply as an owner, whose entitled freedom is
individuated in the objective domain that is respected as the recep-
tacle of one's will. What intentions and notions of the good may
accompany one's ownership are just as incidental to this mode of self-
determination as are the qualities of the property and the needs they

address or any community to which the agents belong. The self-determined character of the owner consists in nothing more than the particular factor in which its will has created a recognizable individuated domain for itself, just as this reality of the owner's freedom has no further significance than being the recognized embodiment of the owner's will. All other natural features and psychological attractions that it may possess are irrelevant to its status as property, which pertains merely to its being the domain of some person's will. If instead the will of the person could not abstract from these particular features, the possession of things would be conditioned by given factors internal and external to the agent, preventing the agent from attaining a self-determined existence, one in which the will alone decides what embodiment to give itself, or, in other words, where what the agent wills is its own realization as self-determined. What allows an agent to determine itself as an owner and acquire something as property is achieving recognition for the externalization of its will in that factor, a recognition that has no reference to the particular natural features of that factor or its relation to need and welfare.[5]

The only limitations upon the content of the factor of property inherent in the self-determination of owners are one, that the objectification of any owner's will not be the reality of another person's will, and two, that the factor in question be something that can exhibit in some recognizable fashion its relation to the will of its putative owner. The first qualification, which excludes persons from appropriation as objects of property, is simply a matter of observing the duty of respecting the right of other persons, which accompanies any self-determination as an entitled owner. The second qualification, which excludes from ownership such entities as unreachable stars and omnipresent forces and particles, is built into the requirement that an entitled exercise of freedom have a determinate reality that is recognizable by others. By contrast, the constitutive freedom of persons is violated by any Lockean provisos that restrict the right to take ownership of unowned factors in respect to how that appropriation adversely affects particular interests of others.[6] Any such limitations subordinate property entitlements to welfare considerations that heed the particularity of need and advantage. These considerations may have their place within civil society, but not within the abstract right of property interaction, which civil society itself incorporates as a necessary ingredient in its market relations.

Accordingly, the right of property does not itself mandate any Jacobin demand for equal ownership or any other specific claim of distributive justice. Although all persons as such do have a right to own property and thereby be free of enslavement, further distributive concerns only arise with more determinate freedoms, such as those of being a family member, entitled to sharing the household property; of being a member of civil society, entitled to equal economic opportunity; or of being a citizen of a constitutional democracy, entitled to equal opportunity for political action.

Nevertheless, even if the recognized freedom of owners leaves largely indeterminate the scope of property, property relations cannot help but invest one particular property with a special primacy that imposes unique restrictions upon its disposal. Both with respect to the order of conception and the order of realization, no factor can be appropriated as property until each person has achieved recognized ownership of his or her own body. The person's own facticity must be taken ownership of first, precisely because otherwise no act of that individual can possibly be recognized as properly that person's own. This ownership, like any other, involves a structure of right and duty where each participant honors the correlative embodiments of the wills of the others in order to enjoy his or her own entitlement. The taking ownership of one's own body is thus an act that operates in conjunction with the same mutual recognitions whereby all other persons appropriate their own facticity. Consequently, persons cannot interact as such without at the same time recognizing each other's exclusive title to his or her own body. Moreover, since no person can exercise any property right or any other right if his or her self-ownership is relinquished, the ownership of one's own body is inalienable.

Self-ownership has posed a dilemma for many theorists in virtue of the apparent reflexivity and inalienability that distinguish it from ownership of other factors. Lockeans, of course, have trouble acknowledging self-ownership without contradicting their labor theory of property, which, besides all its monological limitations, is ill-suited to accommodate proprietorship of a body that can hardly be the product of a labor that must always already employ the body as its primary instrument. To interpret Locke as making individuals owners not of their bodies, but of their persons and actions, provides little remedy.[7] After all, persons and actions can hardly be products of individuals' own labor in any juridical sense if their bodies are not already recognized to be under the dominion of their own wills rather than subject to some other master.

By contrast, self-ownership has been ignored by those, like the young Marx,[8] who, failing to distinguish labor from labor power, overlook how wage laborers cannot be propertyless, since engaging in wage labor rests upon recognition at least as proprietor of one's own labor power, something of which slaves are deprived. Consequently, poverty, under conditions of market economy, is not a matter of propertylessness but of a distinctly economic deprivation.

Yet, if admitted, how can self-ownership be coherently conceived when the owner and property appear to be one and the same? The dilemma would be insoluble if indeed the body inalienably owned by the person were identical to the will it embodies, leaving any would-be act of appropriation grasping at nothing but itself. However, although the body may be the vehicle of every act willed by the person, it may still be distinguished from the volition by which persons lay claim to their facticity and individuate themselves as persons. Otherwise, no distinction could possibly be drawn, for instance, between involuntary and voluntary bodily movements, which may, after all, be physically indistinguishable. Indeed, unless individuals draw such a distinction on their own, they can recognize neither themselves nor others as agents. Hence, strictly speaking, there is no self-ownership proper, for what the self owns is its body, not the will presiding over it.[9] Moreover, although that volition employs both the body and the capacity of choice natural to the will, it only figures as the self-determination of an owner through the interrelation of individuals who recognize their own wills to be objectified in their respective bodies. As with any entitlement, the right to own one's body entails a relation to other persons who have the duty to respect one's self-ownership as well as the right to have their self-ownership respected in turn.[10] Accordingly, in self-ownership, the "self" that is owned is the body, whereas the owner is the person, the artificial agency determining itself in property relations, not the body, nor the natural will comprising the capacity of choice presupposed by each and every decision.[11] For this very reason, slaves and concentration camp inmates can and have been acknowledged to have a body controlled by their own capacity of choice without this involving any juridical recognition of ownership of their body.

If this differentiation of the person, the "natural" will and the body resolves the puzzle of the reflexivity of self-ownership, the inalienability of self-ownership remains a problem for thinkers such as Stephen Munzer,[12] who denies that persons own their bodies because persons allegedly instead have only some limited property rights over their own facticity, much as medieval serfs enjoyed exclusive use of their land without any entitlement to sell it away. What undermines all such claims is the impossibility of enjoying any rights whatsoever unless one's body is concordantly recognized to objectify no will but one's own. Any lesser status removes the basic independence distinguishing free individuals from slaves, precluding any privileged enjoyment of all or any part of one's own body. That persons have no right to sell or destroy their bodies testifies not to how persons do not own their bodies but rather to how any termination of ownership of one's body precludes exercising any right whatsoever. Consequently, contra Munzer,[13] Marx, and others who confuse property and commodity relations, transferability is not the criterion for identifying property ownership, nor can property as such be bound up with buying and selling in the market. Commodities may all be property, but not all property can take the form of a commodity. Any division of body rights into personal rights and property rights, such as Munzer makes,[14] only invites further confusion. Although all rights involve the respected exercise of acts of will involving some employment of one's body, no such exercise can count as one's own without a simultaneous recognition of self-ownership.

Once, however, persons recognize one another as exclusive owner of one's own body, each is in a position to acquire other objects of property, which, in the first instance, are factors not yet embodying the will of any other person.[15] Such unowned factors can present no juridical barriers to appropriation by the first will to obtain recognized embodiment in them since the will of the person can only be limited by the self-determination of others. Accordingly, the move from self-ownership to first occupancy acquisition of other property follows directly, without the need for additional psychological, social, or normative background theory that Munzer, for one, falsely claims to be necessary.[16] However, contrary to the monological terms of first occupancy in Locke, Kant, and other liberal theorists, this "original appropriation" of property must once again operate in terms of the reciprocal recognition in which any right and its correlative duty are constituted.[17] Otherwise, first occupancy reverts to a purely physical relation, whose temporal priority lacks the normative dimension that interrelations among persons alone make possible. Accordingly, each prospective owner must make his or her claim in a recognizable way, whether by physically grasping, altering, or simply marking the factor, that conforms with the complementary claims of those persons from whom respect is awaited.[18]

Since whatever factor recognized as mine becomes subject to my exclusive dominion, persons are entitled to use their property as they see fit so long as in so doing they do not injure or jeopardize the person and property of other owners. Since the rights of persons do not extend to providing for their particular needs and interests but only to upholding the recognized embodiment of their will, use of property does not violate the property rights of others simply by being disadvantageous to their welfare. Although the prerogatives of other spheres of right may permit nuisance in property use to be defined in respect to resulting disadvantage, the rights of ownership do not themselves extend the bounds of wrongful use of property beyond what violates the ownership of others.[19] Subject to this latter more limited proviso, owners are at liberty to use their property by consuming it, leaving it otherwise intact, relinquishing ownership without further qualification, or transferring the use of it for a limited time or the entire ownership of the property to another recognized person. And in the case of transfer of the limited use of or entire ownership of a property, each assignment may be done either as a gift or in exchange for the partial use or exclusive ownership of some other property. All of these options are rights of an owner because curtailing them would make the embodiment of a person's will dependent upon something other than its own self-determination.[20]

Because the ownership of any factor resides in recognition rather than in any physical act or psychological attitude, any alteration in ownership must obtain due recognition. This proviso applies as much to the mere withdrawal from ownership of some property as to any transfer to others of its use or ownership. In the first case, a person relinquishes ownership only through some sufficiently recognizable act that informs other persons that the factor no longer embodies the will of its previous owner. In the latter cases, transfer of use and ownership can only occur if the other party equally wills the transaction in a manner recognizable to other persons in general.

Consequently, whether the alteration of use and ownership take the form of a gift or an exchange for the use or ownership of another's property, the transfer takes the form of a contract, whose participants together will the transfer in question. Once again, since ownership is determined through recognition, what counts is the coming to an agreement of the transfer in title or use, not the physical performance of the transfer, which may or may not be simultaneous with the transfer of ownership or use.[21]

Furthermore, when the contract involves the exchange of properties and/or the use of properties, an equivalence of value is established in the act of exchange that consists in the equation of the exchanged factors agreed to in the transaction. Since the contract is freely entered by each person, the equivalent value of the exchanged properties is a purely arbitrary matter, residing in nothing but the agreement of the parties involved. Any appeal to other determinations of value, based on market relations, psychological attachments, or natural features, would violate the property rights of the parties to the contract by constraining their transactions by factors extraneous to their freedom as owners.[22] From the standpoint of property relations, any questions regarding the value of what is exchanged must thus refer to the representations given in the contractual agreement itself. Although other spheres of right may bring other claims to bear upon the outcome of contracts, all that the right of contract itself mandates is that the parties be capable of comprehending and independently agreeing to the terms of the contract, that the articles exchanged be what they are represented to be, and that the value of the transferred factors count as what they have been exchanged for on that basis. In their capacity as owners, persons are otherwise free of any duties to contract with one another in respect of any specific needs or other welfare considerations, or to enter contract with any particular motivations or expectations other than what pertains to the representation of the terms of their agreement. These conditions of contractual obligation are sufficient to support the traditional principle of no liability for nonfeasance,[23] since they leave the entering into contract to the discretion of persons. Moreover, these conditions equally uphold the doctrine of unconscionability, by which the enforcement of contract heeds the adequacy of exchanged considerations, without any appeal to additional imperatives of distributive justice or any other norms. For if a contract is made without due understanding and willingness on the part of all parties concerned, it subverts its own authority as an agreement realizing its participants' mutual obligation to respect the knowing and willing of one another as owners of property.[24]

Nevertheless, the freedom of contract ingredient in property right does require amendment in respect to the more concrete freedoms of family, civil society and the state. Contrary to Unger,[25] however, such revision does not reflect a contradiction between contractual freedom and community but rather the very terms by which the ethical associations of family, civil society, and state incorporate property right in conformity with the demands of their own modes of self-determination. Since property right is a precondition for self-determined membership in any form of community, the integration of contract within these further spheres is a necessity for the spheres themselves. Hence, that integration can only involve restricting the right of contract in particular ways, rather than obliterating it completely.

The Nonlegal Determination of Wrong

These fundamental features of the self-determination of persons entail a differentiation of violations of property rights, independently of any reference to legality or any other institution of right. In particular, they mandate that the "harm" specific to violations of property right not be tied to welfare, following the utilitarian view for which the harm of wrong lies in "setbacks to interests," to quote Joel Feinberg's rehabilitation of Mill's program.[26] Since determining oneself as an owner is indifferent to one's particular ends, concerning only the external embodiment of one's will in abstraction from any accompanying needs, desires, and motives, violations of property right are equally indifferent to how they affect advantage and disadvantage. The fact that, for example, a theft may ultimately benefit its victim by preventing the latter from boarding an airliner doomed to crash, does not mitigate the wrong consisting in the violation of property right.[27] Moreover, welfare considerations cannot even become matters of entitlement unless violations of persons' property rights already count as wrongs. Contrary to the primacy accorded welfare in utilitarianism, if individuals' self-ownership is violated with impunity, they are virtual slaves, in no position to have their interests respected on a par with others.

What makes wrong possible is simply that all persons have a faculty of choice enabling them to act upon interpretations of particular property entitlements in disagreement with others, to inadvertently harm the person and property of others, and to disregard purposely the property entitlements they recognize, whether openly or furtively, through omission or commission.

Persons may thus be victims of nonmalicious wrongs, where they suffer unauthorized use and/or damage to their property (including their own body) either through unintended, non-negligent actions or accidents involving the property of others or else when others act upon a belief that their action falls within what they interpret to be their rights as owners. In such cases, neither victim nor perpetrator acts in conscious disregard of property rights. Since whatever loss results occurs nonmaliciously, the perpetrator did not will in opposition to right and no punishment is deserved. Instead of involving a general wrong of willing against right, nonmalicious wrong involves a particular violation of ownership revolving around either non-negligent unintended behavior or unintended effects of one's property, or a disagreement in the interpretation of the boundaries of ownership.[28] Given the rights of owners, any recognized injury to a person's property must be duly recompensed, either through restitution of wrongly appropriated property, by replacement of destroyed property, or, when this is impossible, by compensation according to the contractually established value of the irreplaceable property. Moreover, whoever is duly recognized to be responsible for the injury, by either committing the act or being owner of the property causing injury, is responsible for providing due compensation. Persons whose own body or other property is involved in accidental injury and damage are here accountable for damages because they, as owners, are exclusively responsible for the factors over which their will has proprietorship. Moral considerations limiting responsibility to acts done on purpose and to their intended consequences do not already apply to property right. Property relations abstract from purpose and intention except in distinguishing between malicious and nonmalicious wrong, a distinction that serves to identify when punishment, but not compensation, is due. In these respects, nonmalicious wrong presents a model case of strict liability, insofar as compensation is owed victims independently of fault.[29]

The only consideration endemic to property right that enables a person to escape liability for harm tied to their property is if the victim suffered personal injury and/or property damage as a result of committing trespass. In that case, the owner cannot be responsible for what happens to the victim, since the victim's very contact with the offending property violated the will of the owner.

The call to replace tort liability entirely with a social accident insurance scheme ignores the fact that property relations themselves involve no further distributive imperatives nor any institutions authorized to compensate victims that might shift the burden of compensation elsewhere. Admittedly, property relations themselves cannot guarantee that victims of accidental harm will be duly compensated by the responsible parties, and the rights of those victims can only be upheld if compensation is publicly guaranteed. Moreover, the difficulties of employing litigation to enforce tort liability may well provide grounds for introducing no-fault insurance programs simply in order to uphold the rights of victims. However, these considerations do not eliminate the strict liability of nonmalicious wrong, as defined within the elementary context of property relations. They instead point to modifications that ensue when property rights figure within civil society.

The case is different when property rights are violated with malice. Since individuals can suffer consequences involuntarily either through ignorance or force,[30] malicious wrong can occur either through fraud, where the victim is misled about the true character of a particular property transaction, or through outright crime, where the perpetrator makes no show of respecting the victims' rights, but openly violates them, either by directly harming their person or property, by neglecting to take due precautions to avoid reasonably foreseeable risks to their person and property, or by refraining from coming to their aid when doing so does not put one in any commensurate danger.[31]

The victims of malicious wrong are no less due compensation for the violations of their property than victims of nonmalicious wrong. However, the perpetrators are not merely responsible for providing that compensation. Because they have intentionally violated the rights of their victims, either taking advantage of their ignorance, using force, or contributing to foreseeable and unwarranted risks, they are also liable to punishment. Punishment is here mandated because the malicious act of will against right must itself be nullified to complete the restitution of property rights. Otherwise, the explicit wrong is allowed to count, calling into question the whole fabric of right. Since the compensation of the injury already covers the outward dimension of the violation, punishment applies solely to counteracting the willing against right. Consequently, the appropriate form of punishment is to constrain the will of the perpetrator, that is, imprisonment.

Moreover, since punishment addresses the willing against right rather than the particular wrong that requires compensation, it is possible for individuals to be punished for maliciously acting to violate the person and property of others even when no particular harms actually result.[32] Hence, attempted but unsuccessful arson, theft, assault, murder, and so on are punishable crimes.

A similar rationale underlies the criminality of negligence. Admittedly, a perpetrator of negligence does not maliciously commit a particular wrong, but only creates or is otherwise responsible for conditions that the perpetrator knows either lead or are likely to lead to unwarranted harm to someone's person and property. However, by both knowingly participating in the creation of unreasonable risk and failing to remove the danger for which he or she is responsible, the negligent party passes beyond the pale of nonfeasance into the realm of misfeasance.[33] This passage into misfeasance still applies in cases where negligent parties do not knowingly contribute to unreasonable endangerment, but should have known. Then ignorance is no excuse, for they are responsible for their own unawareness and its ramifications. Hence, whether with knowledge or out of inexcusable ignorance, the negligent party in effect wills in express indifference to others' property right, committing a general wrong that stands even if no particular harm occurs. Accordingly, negligence that imperils the person and property of others is punishable simply for unduly jeopardizing the property entitlements of others,[34] rather than for violating any further duty to care for the welfare of others.[35] For although, with respect to property right, negligence consists in a breach of the obligation to honor the personhood and property of others, this still involves no reference to their additional particular interests and welfare.[36] Insofar as the responsibility in negligent conduct is a form of willing against property right, it must be treated as a malicious wrong, for which the malefactor deserves punishment. As in any case of criminal conduct, if negligence leads to actual injuries to persons and damage to property, the perpetrator stands liable for compensation; if no such particular wrong occurs, the malefactor is liable for no damages, but a general wrong remains that mandates punishment.[37]

In effect, all negligence is criminal. For if a person has unknowingly put others in jeopardy without being under any obligation to know any better, that person is no different from an owner whose property occasions accidental harm. In such cases, strict liability for compensation applies, but punishment has no place.

The case of the bad Samaritan is analogous. The bad Samaritan *chooses* not to intervene to help someone whose person is imperiled, fully aware that circumstances make rescue dependent upon his or her personal intervention without imposing great risk.[38] These latter two conditions are crucial. If, on the one hand, the situation does not make the rescue of the victim depend upon the personal initiative of the potential good Samaritan (as in cases of widespread famine, disaster, war, and destitution), as well as provide knowledge of that special relation to the possible rescuer, that individual is no more obliged to intervene than any other. On the other hand, if a potential rescuer risks as much danger as the victim, any "duty" to intervene would cancel the rescuer's right to the same freedom that the victim stands to lose. Moreover, although property right does not oblige owners to guarantee one another any particular type or amount of property (other than exclusive ownership of their body), let alone any further degree of welfare, it does prescribe upholding one another's status as persons, which is precisely what life-threatening emergencies imperil.[39] Hence, the problem of bad Samaritanism arises only when an individual chooses not to rescue a person in mortal danger even when rescue depends upon that particular intervention and its risks are known to be comparatively minor. Through such an act of omission, the bystander maliciously contributes to harm to a person that threatens not just particular damage but destruction of the very possibility of any self-determination whatsoever.[40] Any limited property loss or injury the bad Samaritan might suffer is thus hardly commensurate with the fate awaiting the unaided victim. Knowing yet ignoring this, the bad Samaritan is therefore personally responsible for undermining the property right of another, just as are the criminally negligent who fail to take due precautions that would remove mortal dangers. By failing to rescue the victim, the indifferent spectator thus commits a general wrong calling for punishment, whether or not it is accompanied by a particular wrong for which compensation is due. In this way, bad Samaritanism comprises a case of misfeasance, rather than nonfeasance, allowing for a duty of rescue that does not contradict the generally prohibitive form of obligation in property right. If instead this duty to rescue were based upon welfare considerations, following utilitarian lines,[41] the ethical significance of the distinction between misfeasance and nonfeasance would be threatened since the promotion of advantage need not restrict punishment to fault.[42] Here, however, the distinction remains in force, permitting the freedom of persons to be unimpeached.

Similarly, the classical tort law defense of necessity, which permits someone in peril to take the property of another provided compensation is later furnished, need not be seen to conflict with the rule against liability for nonfeasance.[43] Since the imperiled individual has appropriated property he or she desperately needs, the owner would be acting to undermine the entire personhood of that individual by taking back what the other's life depends upon. That deed would accordingly comprise misfeasance, rather than nonfeasance, and be subject to punishment. By contrast, general emergencies, where personal intervention by certain individuals is not specifically required for rescuing imperiled persons and property, call for a public intervention that fairly imposes burdens upon all individuals while not unfairly singling out some endangered individuals for special help. Such public intervention can be handled by the welfare institutions of civil society, but not by property relations alone or by bringing individual cases to court.[44] Indeed, in the context of civil society, the right to aid extends beyond the survival needs of persons to the further requirements of family well-being and economic opportunity, allowing for possible extensions of good Samaritan duties.

In any case, whether fraud, negligence, bad Samaritan conduct, or outright crime is at issue, punishing malefactors not for having willed against right but to "rehabilitate" them or to deter future criminal action by them or others violates the very rights of criminals as persons. Punishment for the sake of deterrence violates the rights of persons by subjecting them to constraints that are not dictated by any righting of actual wrongs or by the upholding of existing property entitlements. Alternately, punishing persons for the sake of rehabilitation amounts to disrespecting the competence and independence of individuals, incoherently treating them as if they had to be instructed and reformed to be fully capable of right conduct while still holding them responsible for maliciously committing a wrong. Although other spheres of right might provide bases for further considerations entering into the determination of punishment,[45] property relations involve no rationale for punishing a person other than guilt for maliciously having done wrong to another.

The modalities of righting wrong duly applying to malicious and nonmalicious infractions are entailed by property entitlements themselves, independently of moral reflection or any positive law and legal institutions. Nonetheless, by themselves, the constitutive relationships of persons are insufficient either to provide a recognized determination of what wrongs have been committed or to authoritatively determine and guarantee the execution of due compensation and punishment.

In the event of nonmalicious wrong, any assessment of injuries is dependent upon an agreement upon where the boundaries of property lie. Such agreement is precisely what is lacking in those cases of conflicting interpretations where the parties dispute titles to ownership, terms of contract, and the like. Given merely the plurality of persons, the only way wrong can be righted in these cases is if the parties bury their hatchets and come to an agreement, with either the self-proclaimed victims withdrawing their claim in deference to the alleged perpetrators or the latter acknowledging the interpretation of their counterpart and agreeing to make good the violation they have admitted. However, either resolution is purely contingent upon the arbitrariness of the parties involved. Moreover, even when one person admits to having nonmaliciously violated the property of another, they may still disagree over what compensation is due. Since persons are all on an equal footing with regard to interpreting their respective property rights, there is simply no higher authority to which they can appeal when conflict persists. If agreement is reached, the perpetrator may not have sufficient property to compensate the victim, and even if the perpetrator does have sufficient property, there still can be no guarantee that the perpetrator will either be willing or be compelled to deliver due compensation. Success will be purely contingent upon the personal decisions of the interested parties.

Righting malicious wrongs is equally unmanageable on the basis of property relations alone. Again, an assessment of property violations can only be accomplished if prior agreement has established the boundaries of particular property entitlements, something for which no guarantee can be given. Second, an assessment of whether malice accompanied the violation depends once more upon agreement concerning what counts as an authoritative description of the alleged fraud or outright crime. Third, even if the parties involved all agree upon violations and malicious intent, the determination of compensation and punishment is just as subject to controversy as the determination of compensation for nonmalicious wrong. And fourth, even if all parties finally concur upon what compensation and punishment should be provided, the criminal may not be able to provide adequate compensation, or, even if sufficiently doted, may still be unwilling to compensate or to submit to punishment. Consequently, it is still a contingent affair whether the victim receives due desert and the criminal due punishment. And whenever disagreement persists, any attempt to punish an alleged criminal will be liable to interpretattion as a new crime, representing a purely personal act of revenge.

These ramifications are of crucial significance both for the place of law and the form and content of legality. On the one hand, legal relations are not ingredient in the independent, irreducible entitlements of persons and the correlative imperatives for righting violations of property rights. Consequently, the sphere of abstract right is *not* the sphere of legality. Property relations are prerequisite components of every sphere of right, however, and therefore legality will have to incorporate persons within its domain and accommodate the normative principles of their interrelations. Accordingly, legal personality will contain personhood, but only as an element of its own irreducible dimension of freedom. Consequently, the personhood of abstract right is not to be identified with legal personality, contrary to the prevailing practice plaguing liberal theory and most commentaries on Hegel's *Philosophy of Right*. On the other hand, the inability of property relations to succeed in righting the wrongs to which they are inveterately subject provides the prospect that legal relations will be charged with resolving this failing. Whether this charge becomes an occupation, let alone the exclusive occupation, of law will depend, of course, upon the character of the other spheres of right that further intervene.

Implications for the Relation between Each Sphere of Right and Law

These implications for the relation between the abstract right of property relations and legality are indicative of the threefold way in which the determination of each successive sphere of right bears upon the place and form and content of law. First, the specification of each mode of self-determination will indicate whether or not legality is contained within it. Second, this will not only indicate within which spheres of right law properly falls, but also the modes of freedom with which law must cohere no matter what institutional realm it may inhabit. Third, the determination of the spheres of right may entail unresolved problems of justice that call for a legal resolution. In that event, the form and content of law will be determined at least partly in view of that unfinished agenda.

Thus both the place and character of law will be determined in the course of the differentiation of the spheres of right. The immediate question is which mode of freedom follows upon property rights? Systematically speaking, the candidate must incorporate personhood while involving no further rights and duties than those specific to its own interaction. Moreover, the putative sphere of right must be incorporated by all other institutions of freedom that follow. If these requirements are not met, the chosen candidate will presuppose more than property relations, introducing an appeal to factors for which no account has been given.

Can the next sphere of right consist in none other than legality itself? If this were the case, then the imposition of a legal order would be predicated, as in liberal theory, upon nothing but the insecurity in which persons are left when no further institutions are at hand to uphold their property entitlements.

Yet a further nonlegal mode of freedom still intervenes before law takes the stage, a mode of freedom that operates with no other resources than the plurality of persons and manages to insert itself within the interstices of every further sphere of right. This additional precursor of legality is moral autonomy, that mode of freedom in which individuals hold one another accountable for acting with the right purposes and motives in behalf of promoting their respective self-determinations.

Morality without Legality

Morality and legality are commonly counterposed as if their relation exhausted the juxtaposition between law and normative conduct. Yet, with normativity residing in the self-ordered system of the reality of self-determination, morality must take its place as but one mode of freedom among others, whose connection with legality involves only one aspect of the prescriptive dimension of law.

Whereas the property rights of persons comprise an elementary freedom in which agent and self-determination are defined by the immediacy of an external factor recognized as the embodiment of will, morality determines conduct as something mediated by the inner resolve of the subject. Although no further institutions of freedom intervene in delineating moral conduct, persons interact as moral subjects by treating one another not just as owners, whose property warrants respect, but as responsible agents who should be held accountable only for those dimensions of their conduct that are prefigured in the purpose and intention with which they act. In this way, morality enables individuals to determine the very objectivity of their conduct, defining the recognizable portion of their deeds for which they as moral subjects are responsible.

Three factors decide the relation between morality and legality: first, the degree to which moral freedom contains legal relations; second, the degree to which the rights and duties specific to moral autonomy impact upon the conduct of legal affairs; and third, the degree to which moral freedom leaves unresolved the dilemmas of property rights and introduces problems of its own that call for a legal solution. An outline of moral self-determination provides a preliminary basis for deciding these issues.[46]

Since conduct is action done on purpose, and action is accompanied by a motive only insofar as it is purposive, morality in the first instance involves being accountable for that aspect of one's deed that reflects the purpose with which one acts and holding others responsible on the same terms. Any concern with motive is predicated upon this prior recognition of the role of purpose in determining the scope of responsible action. Moral freedom thus minimally involves the right of being accountable only for what one does on purpose and, conversely, the duty of respecting the right of others not to be blamed for those features of their conduct that are not determined by their purpose. Since these aspects of right and duty are coeval, moral autonomy initially entails acting with purposes that conform with others realizing their purposes as the defining border of their self-determination. To the degree that acting on purpose is tantamount to attempting to realize one's ends and that achieving one's ends is a general recipe for attaining happiness, the rudimentary moral right to be held responsible only for what one does on purpose provides a nonteleological underpinning to the utilitarian credo that individuals act to promote the happiness of all. As an expression of the right and duty of moral agents holding one another accountable for what their purposes anticipate in their deeds, this principle is simply ingredient in the moral dimension of freedom and thus has a foundation-free legitimacy.

Significantly, the right and duty of defining conduct in terms of the purpose with which it is undertaken incorporates no posited rules nor any public machinery of application and enforcement. Moral agents can act to respect one another's responsibility for their purposive conduct simply by personally restricting their own actions and personally judging their respective accountability. Law need not enter. However, law can conceivably draw the line that individuals should not cross when it comes to holding others responsible for their deeds. Moreover, although the right to be held responsible does not itself mandate any positive purposes, it does prescribe the negative stricture to choose one's purpose so that it neither holds other individuals accountable for what they do inadvertently nor hinders them from achieving purposes that do not interfere with the like activity of others. Whether law is needed to provide this service and whether this involves something more than enforcing the rights of persons are other matters, determined by the outcome of the further dimensions of moral freedom.

The second dimension of moral autonomy, which presupposes how purpose is recognized to determine the scope of responsibility, centers upon motive as a factor of self-determination. Whereas individuals act with purpose, they choose a particular purpose because of an underlying motive, anticipating desired ramifications of the intended course of action. Since any deed not only involves aspects extending beyond the action achieving the purpose of the agent but also ramifications that are incidental to those motivating the chosen purpose of the act, individuals remain self-determined in their conduct only insofar as they are held responsible exclusively for those ramifications of what they purposely do that correspond with their motivating intention.

Otherwise, the deed associated with their agency remains stamped with extraneous features that undermine it as a realization of the agent's freedom. Accordingly, moral subjects exercise a further dimension of autonomy to the extent that they recognize each other's accountability as extending solely to the consequences of conduct that are prefigured in the motive underlying the choice of purpose. Given the reciprocity of right, exercising the right to be responsible only for what one has intended as the motive of one's intentional action equally involves acting to honor the same right on the part of all other moral subjects. Consequently, to the degree that moral agents determine the ramifications of their actions as their own responsibility in reference to their own motives, they enjoin themselves to act with motives that can be acted upon in conformity with all other moral agents doing the same. This constitutive feature of how the determination of responsibility figures in moral interaction in light of motive supplies the basic formula of the categorical imperative. Significantly, it supervenes upon the universal promotion of happiness ingredient in the right of purpose without eliminating the former.

Once more, the resulting right and duty of being responsible for only the ramifications of conduct that one intends involves no positing of public rules nor any public authority for applying and enforcing them in particular cases. Individuals can hold one another accountable in function of their motives as well as in function of their purposes simply by acting with purposes and motives they deem compatible with the like conduct of others and by judging the responsibility of their counterparts in the same way that they would judge their own.

Nevertheless, although individuals may be able to autonomously determine their conduct by holding themselves and others accountable for those aspects of action and its consequences that conform to the agent's purposes and for those motives that accompany them, the purposes and motives moral agents should give themselves remain undetermined. Consequently, each moral subject faces the additional task of determining the right purposes and motives to act upon. Given that moral agency addresses this undertaking as part of its own autonomy rather than as something already settled by externally existing conventions, it operates as conscience, determining by itself the content of good aims and motives. However, because enjoying this moral freedom as a right involves recognizing the entitlement of every other moral agent to do the same, each individual falls into a moral quandary for which nothing but a purely incidental, evanescent escape is to be had with the resources provided by moral interaction. On the one hand, each moral agent is obliged to act with purposes and motives that should have universal validity and thereby warrant respect by all other moral agents. On the other hand, if a moral subject is to acknowledge another subject's right to determine with equal autonomy which purposes and motives are good, a twofold dilemma arises. If the purpose and motive sanctioned by another individual's conscience differ from those of one's own, then one can honor the freedom of conscience of the other moral subject only by acknowledging the validity of the other's purpose and motive at the expense of the claims of one's own conscience. Alternately, if one upholds the universal validity of one's own purpose and motive, then one must rescind one's respect of the authority of the conflicting conscience of the other moral subject. The only way out of this conundrum is if the consciences of different moral subjects happen to arrive at compatible determinations of good purposes and motives. Yet, insofar as each moral agent enjoys freedom of conscience by independently determining what purpose and motive should be had, any concordance between the conscience of agents will be purely arbitrary and devoid of any guaranteed durability. The very autonomy of moral agency precludes the "preestablished harmony" that would be needed to surmount the dilemma.

As a result, as much as morality may enjoin individuals to personally initiate the realization of right by acting with good purposes and motives, the endemic discrepancy of consciences prevents moral agency from either resolving the dilemmas afflicting property relations or arriving at actions that unambiguously realize the moral freedom of all. With regard to legality, this outcome signifies that righting violations of property entitlements remains an abiding task for which law might be recruited. Does it also mean, however, that law may be called upon to resolve the conflicts of moral agents by establishing a harmonious determination of valid purposes and motives for conduct?

Traditionally, legality has been barred from any such undertaking for the simple reason that something as inward as purposes and motives cannot be externally regulated. Only actions can be subject to legal regulation. Law may well be enjoined to treat violations of rights in function of the purposes and motives that accompany them, such as in discriminating between cases of malicious and nonmalicious wrong.

Yet this injunction does not mean that law can mandate with what aims and intentions agents should act. Legality still confines its regulation to the field of external action, even if violations of right deserve punishment only when they are established to be accompanied by malicious intent. As for actions that do not violate right, their accompanying purpose and motive are matters for moral judgment rather than legal adjudication.

Admittedly, the independence of moral reflection always makes it possible for conscience to conflict with legality, as well as with any other institution. Not only may action in accord with the law be performed with immoral purpose and intention, but conscience may well dictate illegal conduct. Nevertheless, legality can regulate the external relations of individuals in a way that conforms to the basic imperatives of moral responsibility. On the one hand, the legal order can realize the right of moral agents to achieve purposes of their own choosing in conjunction with one another by enforcing the public welfare through affording equal economic opportunity to the members of a regulated market. In this respect, legality can provide a solution to the utilitarian injunction to promote the happiness of all on an equal footing. On the other hand, by enforcing the formal rights of persons, legality can provide a system in which the universalizability of action is upheld, regardless of the substantive ends that are pursued. In this way, legality can corroborate the deontological imperative to respect the dignity of individuals by enforcing conditions of conduct under which agents must follow a lawful course of action, which is self-imposed provided legal subjects exercise the political prerogative of being the author of laws they obey.[47]

Moreover, legality will be part of the solution to the quandaries of moral autonomy to the degree that law consists in a form of ethical community. Ethical community provides the compatibility of aims and intentions that moral interaction can never guarantee precisely because participating in ethical association involves exercising a role defined in terms of the pursuit of common ends already embodied in the institutional framework that constitutes that role. Thus, for example, citizens can only exercise their political freedom to the extent that they recognize in common the constitutional framework of self-government within which their political freedom can alone operate and which itself consists in nothing but the common exercise of that freedom. If legality comprises a mode of ethical association, then legal subjects will exercise their legal rights only insofar as they act in common recognition of the authority of legal institutions and of what counts as valid law. Participating in legal relations will then automatically involve a certain degree of conformity in aim, free of the discrepancies plaguing conscience.

In all these respects, morality provides normative agendas awaiting legal implementation even if the external regulation of a legal order can never effectively extend to any positive prescription of purposes and intentions. Furthermore, given morality's own inability to unambiguously determine which purposes and motives are good or to guarantee the external fulfillment of its own inner resolves, the upholding of property rights remains an abiding challenge fit for a legal solution.

Does this signify, however, that legality follows upon property rights and morality as an institution bound to respect person and moral accountability but otherwise predicated upon no further normative relations? Once more, the answer depends upon whether there are any further structures of freedom that neither presuppose nor contain legality within their own workings. Two institutions immediately intervene, provided that they are constituted as spheres of self-determination: the family and the market.

The family precedes the market both in the order of conception and in the order of realization since the market incorporates families and their members, whereas the very unity of the household excludes market relations as a characteristic interaction between spouses, siblings, and parents and their children. Moreover, although market participants need not be married or parents, family life becomes an obstacle to any universal exercise of economic opportunity unless household relations enable spouses to retain an equal autonomy. As a consequence, the household is conceivable and realizable apart from and prior to the market, just as both are conceivable and realizable apart from and prior to legality.

The Family as Antecedent to Legality

Given the normativity of self-determination, the family takes its place as a valid association only when it is structured as an institution of freedom. And only when the household is conceived in its legitimate form can the valid relation between the family and legality be determined.

Conceiving the family as an institution of freedom might appear problematic owing to how factors given independently of willing, such as gender, sexual orientation, and the biology of reproduction and birth, have historically played a determining role in defining household relations. Yet just as the facts of given convention cannot prescribe how conduct should be ordered, so the historical configurations of the family do not mandate the anatomy of the free household.

Minimally speaking, the family involves a relation between spouses or a relation between parent and child. For the former relation to be an association of a specific mode of self-determination, the spouses must be bound to one another through their own free agreement as independent agents, irrespective of extraneous factors such as parental approval, differences of race and hereditary rank, or any cultural matters that would restrict their choice. Moreover, the freedom to form a family cannot be excluded in reference to such naturally conditioned factors as procreation, gender, or sexual orientation. Whether or not prospective spouses are physically able or willing to produce children has no more bearing on their right to form a family together than whether they are of the same gender or of a certain sexual orientation. What counts is their capacity to engage in the acts of will whereby they associate into a common home and take on the rights and duties that go together with being spouses responsible for one another's right and welfare. The home in which they join together is not to be identified with the physical reality of a particular dwelling but rather with the juridical association of a single private domain in which spouses share their property and well-being. Hence, individuals may well live apart yet still retain the rights and duties vis-à-vis one another that form the family bonds defining them as spouses.

The act of marriage whereby individuals become spouses must, like any entitled relation, have a recognizable reality such that the spouses themselves and other individuals are in a position to understand when the association of a common home has been established, investing its specific rights and duties upon the marriage partners. As such, the marriage agreement sets its participants in a twofold position, as spouses in a relation to one another and as representatives of their family in relation to others. Each relation involves its corresponding rights and duties in function of the special normative association marriage establishes.

Although marriage incorporates property relations within its bounds, it is not simply reducible to a special form of contract, where, to paraphrase Kant, spouses simply agree to exchange exclusive use of each other's bodies. Spouses certainly may enter into prenuptial agreements that leave them facing one another as independent property owners with respect to part of their holdings, but unless the marriage creates a single domain of privacy, whose participants have joined together as a united person with a common household property and welfare, the would-be spouses remain mere housemates or friends without any specific rights and duties beyond the imperatives of morality and respect of property that apply to strangers.

The occasion for becoming spouses is a mutual agreement, proceeding minimally from nothing but a common feeling to marry, which need not conform to any particular erotic, romantic, or otherwise psychological model of love. This common feeling can be said to persist within the marriage as an ethical love[48] to the degree that it comprises the disposition to fulfill one's duties as spouse. These duties involve honoring one's spouse's rights to be an equal partner in the management of household affairs, including the use and disposal of household property, and to have his or her welfare treated with equal care and attention. Although spouses may agree to play different particular roles in attending to household chores and representing the family welfare in relation to the society of other individuals, such differences have legitimacy only insofar as the spouses have freely agreed to so apportion their responsibilities and opportunities. Exercising such household rights and duties has nothing to do with differences of gender, sexual orientation, or anything else extraneous to the acts of will involved, and marriage therefore cannot be legitimately restricted by such normatively irrelevant factors.

In their relations to other persons and their property, spouses may certainly engage in contractual relations. However, the rights of spouses to one another set a limit to what one spouse can do with the family property without consulting the other. Moreover, with the incidental exception of prenuptial agreements that affect only those properties that fall outside the unity of the home, spouses cannot properly engage in full-fledged contractual relations with one another regarding the common domain they share. Only when the marriage breaks apart does the shared household property legitimately become subject to contractual relations between independent persons.[49]

Although children are not a necessary feature of the family, marriage partners may assure the further role of parents, which, like any normative relation, is rooted not upon biological ties but upon recognized acts of will. Spouses become the recognized parents of children that are their biological offspring only insofar as they assume the responsibility of fulfilling their duties as parents. Given the normativity of freedom, this responsibility consists in nothing other than bringing up their children to become autonomous individuals, fit and able to assume the entitled roles of person, moral subject, and prospective spouse. Until children reach a maturity measured in respect to reaching the point of exercising the various modes of autonomy that comprise being an independent property owner, moral subject, member of civil society, and citizen, parents have a tutelary guardianship over them, the right to which they lose either when they fail to meet its responsibilities or when the child attains maturity. Since exercising the duties of parent has no necessary relation to any biological tie to children, individuals may become the recognized parents of children that are adopted, just as individuals who fail to honor their parental responsibility to their offspring forfeit their right to remain their guardian. Once again, exercising the right and duty of parent has nothing to do with gender, sexual orientation, racial identity, or any relation to the child extraneous to the capacity to be duly responsible. No matter what the identity of parents and their children, if they are bound together as members of the same family, they are all entitled to have their welfare be treated as a common concern.

If spouses are to withdraw from their marriage legitimately, they must do so in accord with honoring their respective duties to share the common property of the family and to provide for the welfare of one another and their children. By contrast, when children reach maturity, they no longer owe their parents the obedience required by their upbringing to autonomy, and their parents no longer owe them the care and subsistence they were due as children. Consequently, family freedom is incompatible with traditional extended households where elders continue to exercise authority over adult children and the latter's spouses and offspring.

This outline of the rights and duties specific to a family reconstructed as an association of self-determination entails important ramifications for the role and content of law. To begin with, the association of the family does not itself contain legal institutions as part of its own interaction. The interrelated acts of will constitutive of marriage and parental relations can all operate independently of law. Yet, like property relations, the ethical bonds of the family cannot themselves be counted upon to resolve the conflicts and violations to which they are inveterately subject. Spouses can always maliciously violate their duties to one another and their children. The mere plurality of families offers no remedy other than in the contingent and resistible initiative of the injured parties themselves or in that of private individuals outside the home. Even when action on the part of family members or outsiders is forthcoming, such interventions are liable to interpretation as further wrongs in the absence of any recognized authority to certify what wrongs have been committed and what compensation and punishment should be meted out. The situation is no better when spouses nonmaliciously wrong each other or their children through unintentional acts or by simply disagreeing over how to manage household affairs. Unless the spouses can reach agreement, such disputes remain just as intractable as any malicious violations of family rights. Consequently, although law is not itself an ingredient in family relations, legality may well have a role to play in enforcing family rights and duties if no further institutions of freedom intervene to resolve the matter. In that case, a domain of family law, distinct from simple property law, will be called for, addressing all those aspects of family freedom that are subject to external regulation. Law may not be able to command individuals to love one another or have any other inner passion. Yet, since the ethical love animating the family is bound up with the activities of honoring the rights and duties of spouses and children, the imperatives of family freedom can fall within the scope of the law.

Although the upholding of family right may depend upon legality, the free family is itself a prerequisite for the realization of legal order as well as of a free civil society and democratic state. If family relations are structured independently of household self-determination, with spouses neither entering marriage freely nor thereupon codetermining household affairs and sharing equally in caring for one another's welfare, some family members become oppressed by others, obstructing equal participation in the economic, legal, or political opportunities that market freedom, legality, and self-government are to provide to all. Hence, although participants in markets, legal practice, and politics need not be married or parents, the household will be incompatible with these further spheres of right, which otherwise can incorporate duly ordered families within themselves, unless the family is structured as an institution of freedom.

Does legality then follow upon the family in the order of the concept of right, coming upon the scene enjoined both to respect the independently determined rights possessed by legal persons as owners, moral subjects, and family members and to employ law in enforcing rectitude on their behalf? Such would be the case if all further institutions of freedom presuppose and/or incorporate legality. However, just as the family can build a particular association of self-determination without containing legality, so civil society contains at least two structures of freedom that function independently of law. The market comprises the first of these structures, building the minimal institution of civil society within which individuals interact in pursuit of self-chosen particular ends that can only be realized by contributing to the complementary realization of the analogous ends of others. On the basis of participating in the market's web of interdependence, where individuals exercise the opportunity to decide what commodities to need and how to earn a living in reciprocity with others, individuals are also in a position to join together into social interest groups making common cause to fulfill the particular ends they share. In both cases, individuals engage in a specific mode of civil freedom with its own rights and duties, all of which proceeds without any necessary engagement in legal relations. Nevertheless, the very independence of these engagements once more gives legality a two-pronged mandate, whose character can be gleaned from an outline of the parameters of market freedom.

The Market before the Law

Whereas the family can figure as an association of freedom, particular in scope and uniting its members into a single domain of privacy with a shared interest and welfare, civil society comprises a community of particular interests whose web of interdependency is universal in dimension. In order for interests to have a civil character and to serve as the determining factors in the self-determination of individuals, they must consist in particular ends that are given neither simply by nature nor by psychological necessity. To escape such heteronomy, ends must comprise aims whose content is mediated by the will of individuals who determine their agency as a specific mode of freedom in acting to achieve those ends. If the ends in question are, on the one hand, determined by the individual, yet, on the other hand, attainable only by enabling other individuals to realize self-chosen ends of their own, then they mold a community in which individuals relate to one another by pursuing a freely chosen personal interest tied to realizing the same exercise of freedom on the part of others. Far from being a monadic egotism engendering a war of all against all in a state of nature, such an interrelated freedom of interest will proceed only in the context of that specific structure of interdependence which itself consists in individuals pursuing particular ends of their own choosing in reciprocity with one another. Accordingly, this association establishes a form of agency that is determined by its own exercise of will, an exercise conjoining the right of pursuing particular ends of one's own choosing with the duty of respecting the right of others to do the same. Such a freedom of interest operates solely within an existing society of interdependent individuals whose self-chosen ends are already mediated by their relation to one another, so that no participant can realize his or her end without honoring another's right to do the same. Consequently, although each end is self-chosen and particular in scope, the association of interest to which it belongs is an ethical community, building a civil society whose members enjoy the right to pursue their personal self-selected aims in virtue of belonging to an association whose interdependent network already embodies that freedom. [50]

A particular end that has the civil character of being attainable only in reciprocity with the achievement by others of their own self-chosen ends is none other than the need for commodities. Because commodities can only be obtained under the condition of satisfying in exchange the complementary need of their owner, the need for commodities can only be satisfied by providing in return a commodity of one's own that satisfies that owner's respective need. Accordingly, the basic activity of the community of interest of civil society is the commodity exchange of the market, wherein individuals enjoy the right to satisfy needs of their own choosing provided they thereby satisfy the complementary needs of someone else. This activity is able to build a system of its own, liberated from the shackles of a naturally defined subsistence, by grounding commodity exchange upon a self-renewing commodity production, where the factors of production are themselves commodities obtained through exchange and where commodity production and exchange for the sake of accumulating wealth provides an underpinning to a conventional livelihood limited more by the social necessity of the market than by any direct stricture of nature.[51]

Thereby uniting exchange and production, market relations incorporate property relations, with the qualification that property here functions as a commodity, related to the interrelated need of market participants, just as contract here figures in reference to the economic activities of production and exchange.[52] Contrary to the economic determinism of base-superstructure schemas in Marxist thought, commodity relations presuppose rather than engender property entitlements. Without individuals coming to market with goods that they are already recognized to own, commodity exchange cannot even begin to occur. However, just as the plurality of owners lacks the resources to right malicious or nonmalicious violations of property entitlements, so market activity cannot alone uphold the property relations it incorporates. Before, during, and after every commodity transaction and every engagement in commodity production, market participants are liable to suffer unintended injuries and losses and fall into well-intentioned conflicts over the interpretation of their contractual obligations and property holdings, just as they are vulnerable to fraud and outright crime. In no case can the mere workings of the market provide a remedy, for every further commodity transaction is subject to the very same difficulties.

By the same token, market activity cannot itself compel participants to uphold their family rights and duties. However family members may buy, sell, and produce commodities, their economic engagements leave undetermined whether they violate the domestic rights and welfare of their spouses and children, with or without malice.

Moreover, market interaction introduces its own unresolved problems of right, over and beyond the abiding difficulties plaguing property relations and the family. Although every market transaction involves a pair of commodity owners satisfying their self-selected needs in conjunction with one another through activities open in principle to every recognizable person, nothing guarantees that all entitled agents will have an opportunity to exercise their market rights. Not only is it always possible that an individual lacks the commodities that others need, but that person may be unable to find affordable commodities suiting his or her wants or buyers or prospective employers willing to come to terms. Moreover, differences in commodity ownership continually generated by market transactions can always engender new advantages or disadvantages to further market participation, impeding individuals' ability to earn a conventional standard of living through an occupation of their own choice in reciprocity with others. Furthermore, market activity may leave completely unattended the furnishing of all kinds of public goods and infrastructure on which economic well-being depends, and it may undermine the conditions of economic freedom by directly despoiling the environment and ruining public health. In all these respects, commodity exchange and production introduces impediments to the very economic autonomy that requires markets for its exercise.

To a degree, social interest group activity can aim to ameliorate these difficulties. Individuals who share a particular economic interest, whether as consumers, employees, or employers, can use the added force of their collective bargaining power to persuade other market agents on whom they depend to deal with them on more favorable terms, to provide for needed public goods, and to otherwise protect the natural conditions of economic welfare. Yet, no matter how successfully it may monopolize a prized economic factor, such a group can never eliminate the interdependency to which the market condemns all its participants. Even when other economic agents have no other source to which to turn, the outcome may just as well be general economic ruin as irresponsible extortions benefiting few in the short run and none in the long run. Consequently, social interest groups can no more guarantee the success of their efforts to promote the welfare of their members than they can guarantee that individuals outside their group will benefit. Moreover, social interest groups cannot insure that they themselves are free of discriminatory policies, corruption, or other practices that violate the rights of their members.

These limitations persist even if interest groups take advantage of an existing system of civil law protecting the person and property of market agents. Legal enforcement of property and household rights can only uphold the existing distribution of wealth among families, which serves neither to remedy economic disadvantage nor to insure that economic activity provides needed public goods and maintains environmental and public health in the service of equal economic opportunity.

On all these counts, markets and their interest-group extensions engender violations of social rights that their own civil activities are incapable of resolving, even if complemented by a legal system limited to enforcing property or family rights. Since these violations of social freedom pertain not to factors of inwardness eluding legal regulation but to the external economic affairs of individuals and enterprises, legality will face the challenge of widening the scope of its jurisdiction beyond property and family law to a domain of economic law that will enforce the economic freedom and welfare of its legal subjects.

Because this imperative lies in enforcing economic freedom in conformity with the demands of the other spheres of right, it is hardly the source of a legitimation crisis, where public intervention is condemned to undermine its own principles of authority.[53] This crisis would only arise if right was restricted to property entitlements or if public regulation of the market in pursuit of equal economic opportunity imposed not merely particular, but total restrictions on ownership or economic autonomy. Since markets are constitutive of an economic freedom incorporating property relations yet involving more than ownership, market regulation in the service of equal economic opportunity is a pillar of legitimation on which the fate of contemporary regimes will continue to depend.

The Abiding Question: Is There Law in Civil Society or Is Legality Purely an Affair of State?

Owing to the normativity of freedom, the unification of the different spheres of right must be accomplished by an institution of freedom that incorporates them in conformity with its own self-determination. This requirement provides the mandate for the self-grounding sovereign institution of political freedom, which can uphold the prepolitical spheres of right without affront to its own autonomy provided these spheres comprise the preconditions of political autonomy. That they do is readily evident, for if individuals do not enjoy the autonomy of being a recognized owner of property, a morally accountable agent, a free family member, or a market agent enjoying equal economic opportunity, they suffer from forms of bondage hardly compatible with the independence required for political freedom. Yet granted that the freedoms of property relations, morality, the family, and civil society are preserved and consummated within the self-ordered whole of the constitutional democratic state, where does legality finally reside?

Although law will have to conform to the rights of owners, moral subjects, family members, and market participants, the limited resources of their interactions already indicate that legality lies elsewhere. Property owners fall into conflicts of malicious and nonmalicious wrong that they cannot objectively rectify precisely because the recognition process of ownership lacks any authoritative rulings and enforcements of property rights. Since moral agents hold one another accountable for acting with the right purpose and intentions, regardless of any externally given conventions, legality has no more role in morality than any other institution. The family, given its particular scope and basis in an ethical love, has no machinery either for containing legality in the home or for upholding its own household rights in an objectively recognized way. Nor does the market or interest group activity incorporate legal process or any other means for either remedying unresolved violations of property and family rights or for guaranteeing the universal exercise of economic freedom.

By contrast, because the state rules over all other institutions of freedom, shaping and securing them in conformity with its own exercise of self-government, politics cannot help but be occupied with legal affairs if law has any place in valid conduct. But will legality itself be essentially political in character, such that no aspect of law can be conceived or realized apart from political institutions?

Certainly any dimensions of legality predicated upon legislation and constitutionality will have to be considered as part of the determination of the just state. But do all aspects of law issue upon statutory enactment and constitutional authorization?

Alternately, can the just state's rule over prepolitical institutions operate without there being some legal institutions over which government presides, institutions that, since they cannot be incorporated in property ownership, moral striving, the home or the market, must fit within the only other field available, the universal community of interest of civil society as it extends beyond mere commodity relations? Can valid political association even be conceivable, let alone realizable, if legality cannot have an antecedent existence in civil society, this one remaining prepolitical sphere in which it might have a home?

With law framed by the spheres of right, no question turns out to be more central to legal philosophy than this: does legality fall exclusively within the scope of politics, or is there law in civil society?

3 · Civil Society as the Arena of Legality

To determine whether legality resides exclusively within the state or falls also within civil society, it is necessary to identify the social and/ or political preconditions that underlie law as well as to establish the degree to which legality structurally incorporates social and/or political factors. If the minimal specifications of legality can be captured with social, but without any political, ingredients, then the place of law in civil society will be secured.

Heuristic Ramifications of Conceiving Law in Civil Society

One way of addressing these questions is to consider how legality would be determined if it were situated within civil society. This approach can shed light both on what dimensions of legality are components of social freedom but independent of political interaction and upon what aspects of legality figure as preconditions of political association.

Given the structure of social freedom, situating legality within its context would place legal practice as one of four institutional structures of civil society, accompanying market relations on the one hand and the public welfare administration and economic interest group activity on the other. As an institution of civil society, legality would further figure as an element of one of the three modes of ethical community, preceded by the ethical community of the family and followed by that of the state. Taking into account the more global division of the institutions of freedom into those of property rights, morality, and ethical community, legality would be preceded by the structures of property entitlements and moral autonomy.

This ordering departs from the traditional placements of legality in several key ways. Although, like liberal theory, it introduces legality subsequent to the analysis of property relations and morality, it conceives the administration of law only after determining the ethical community of the family and market relations. Moreover, whereas liberal theorists treat law in conjunction with the political activities of civil government, the analysis of legality is here demarcated from political relations, separated by the intermediary institutions of public welfare agencies and economic interest groups. Although the legislative activity of parliamentary organs and the workings of constitutionality within the context of the institutions of political freedom would be subsequently analyzed as part of the conception of the state, these political dimensions of law would remain predicated upon the preceding account of legality in civil society over which they preside as a subordinate prepolitical factor. Conversely, whereas this ordering follows the teleological praxis theory of Plato and Aristotle in prefacing legal theory by an analysis of the household and markets, it departs from the ancients by situating legal practice within the ethical community of interest of civil society, a sphere given no separate normative standing in the classical scheme of *oikos* and *polis*.

Since, systematically speaking, no topic can be legitimately treated before its conceptual prerequisites and antecedently realizable components have been accounted for, the path of legal analysis will necessarily reflect how the various aspects of law are structurally integrated. Given the resultant wedding of form and content in systematic philosophy, the conceptual ordering of legal affairs within the philosophy of right will determine what legality is conceived to be. The placement of legality among the institutions of freedom of civil society should thus be reflected in how legal affairs are themselves conceived.

Four broad ramifications can be anticipated. First, insofar as legality falls within ethical community, whose conception follows upon that of property rights and morality, legal affairs will presuppose property relations and moral subjectivity as necessary structural components. The administration of law will accordingly involve legal subjects who already interact in terms of property rights and moral responsibility, which owe their own determination to features of self-determination given independently of what is simply legal.

These implications have an obvious rationale. The independence of property relations from legality is evident in how the arbitrariness infecting the respect of property claims among owners leaves them open to nonmalicious and malicious wrong, calling for the *addition* of an objectively recognized authority to adjudicate violations, punish offenders, and compensate victims. This need could only arise if property rights were at hand, albeit in an insecure predicament, prior to any legal stipulation and enforcement. Similarly, the independence of morality from legality is evident in how morality enjoins individuals to act with the right purpose and intention irrespective of prevailing institutions. Accordingly, conscience need no more appeal to positive law to determine moral duty than conform to what is legal. Nevertheless, individuals can hardly interact as bearers of legal rights if they are not recognized as property owners or as morally responsible agents. Deprived of property rights, individuals are liable to enslavement; deprived of moral accountability, they are stripped of the competence they must be recognized to have to stand trial and utilize legal process.

Second, although legality will therefore presuppose property relations and moral autonomy, it will transcend their limits by involving a mode of self-determination exhibiting the basic structure of ethical community. Two correlative features distinguish the freedom of ethical community from the self-determinations constitutive of property and morality. On the one hand, the normatively valid end or good at which ethical agency aims contains within itself the activity of its realization. Consequently, ethical agency pursues its constitutive good only by performing a role that is part of what it seeks to achieve. Since this applies to all ethical agents belonging to the community in question, the good they seek is a common one, existing objectively as an institution to which they belong by fulfilling roles that reproduce the very framework in which one can alone be obliged and entitled to perform them. Accordingly, on the other hand, the end to which ethical duty binds is always already actual, existing in the bonds of community upon which such duty is predicated.

This situation contrasts most starkly with the predicament of moral agency, which constitutively acts in reference to a good that is an ought-to-be awaiting both the determination of its content and its realization through the inner resolve of the moral subject.[1] Whereas moral agency is thereby free to operate in any surroundings involving a plurality of responsible individuals, it is inveterately plagued by discrepancies in how each conscience determines the good. By contrast, the rights and duties of ethical community only apply within a framework where practices already operate in recognition of them. This conjunction between the ethical obligation to achieve what ought to be and acting on the basis of its prior realization further reveals how the end of ethical conduct contains the activity of its realization. Nothing reflects this conjunction more plainly than how individuals can enjoy the rights of free citizenship only as members of an existing self-governing state sustained by their exercise of political freedom, or how individuals can exercise their economic freedom only by participating in an existing market system in which the economic opportunity of others is equally realized as the outcome of each transaction.

Legality, determined as a mode of ethical community, will consequently exhibit a similar marriage of "ought" and "is," where the rights of legal agency will apply only within an objectively recognized legal system already realizing the very rights by whose exercise it is reproduced. This situated character of legal agency is reflected in the commonly acknowledged relation between the efficacy and legitimacy of law, as well as in the doctrine of desuetude, according to which a habitually unenforced law loses its authority. Although law retains its binding character independently of whether it is observed in any particular case, it loses its efficacy and thereby ceases to have any obligatory stature if a sufficient number of legal subjects do not recognize the law's authority. In other words, unless legality already exists in the prevailing recognition of the members of the legal community, they cannot interact in terms of legal rights and duties.

Third, to the extent that legality falls in the first instance within civil society, the sphere of ethical community intermediary between the family and the state, legal affairs will manifest what is specific to this particular ethical domain. Legality will thus involve individuals already enjoying household rights and duties and economic opportunities determined independently of legal practice, yet minimally involve nothing specific to political activity. Although law will take on a further political modification through the workings of constitutionality and legislative activity, legality will still retain a civil dimension that is given independently of and prior to what political association adds to legal order. Only then can sense be made of how noncitizens can be subject to the law and participate in legal institutions, or of how there can be nonstatutory common law existing independently of any political enactment. Moreover, although international law ordinarily involves treaties between states, thereby presupposing politics, the possibility of laws indifferent to political boundaries rests upon legality having a dimension given apart from political legislation and constitutionality. That dimension is intimated by such laws as those appealed to under the rubric of "human rights" even in cases of individuals whose nations have not acknowledged them by treaty.

Fourth, to the degree that the administration of law figures as the civil institution intermediary to market relations on the one hand and economic interest group activity and the public administration of welfare on the other, legality will involve legal subjects already exercising their economic freedoms without yet addressing the further concerns of assuring the economic welfare of all. This qualification does not prevent law from extending its reach to matters of social welfare and politics and becoming modified within the practices specific to the administration of welfare and the state. It simply signifies that the administration of law has a character of its own presupposed by these further dimensions of justice, and, therefore, such social and political transformations of law are themselves only conceivable and actualizable on the basis of the antecedent determination of legality in its own right. This implication will be true not only because civil legality is incorporated by other civil institutions and political association. The very limitations of "civil" law will themselves dictate how law must be further modified both to guarantee the realization of social freedom[2] and to conform to the requirements of political self-determination.

Can the concept of law remain true to these ramifications of a placement of legality within civil society, and, more important, does this matter shed light on how legal reality should be ordered?

The Presuppositions of Legality

If legality must be conceived as the second sphere of civil society, presupposing market interaction together with the property, moral, and family relations that economic freedom itself incorporates, law should owe its minimal character to the resources these structures of right already provide without introducing anything dependent upon the welfare, corporate, and political institutions whose conception supposedly follows that of legality. The most elementary determination of legality, incorporated in all further aspects of law, must therefore be determined on the basis of the market institutions of economic autonomy.

The rationale for this stricture might seem to lie in how the administration of law appears to arise out of the external necessity of protecting the commodity ownerships and commercial transactions at play in the market.[3] The fact that the market requires legality to uphold the property entitlements on which commodity relations are predicated is not, however, the key to understanding why legality follows conceptually upon the market.

As is true throughout systematic argument, preceding determinations do not figure as determining principles of what follow from them. If they did, the conceptual development would be foundation-ridden, ultimately resting upon an assumed first principle that would ground all that follows. Any such first principle would fall victim to the dilemmas of foundational justification, where validity consists in being determined by a privileged factor that itself cannot enjoy the same validity without canceling its own priority. This problem can be avoided if the preceding determinations figure not as grounding principles but as the necessary components out of which those factors that follow can be conceived, doing so without determining the latter's new, irreducible character. Then, the resultant structure incorporating all the antecedent elements provides the key to their systematic interconnection, not as something presupposed apart, but in its own constitution as the whole in which they have their ultimate realization.

Accordingly, in the case at hand, the concept of legality follows from that of markets not because the market economy requires legality to uphold its transactions but rather because law minimally involves a mode of interaction, aspects of which are brought into existence through commodity relations. In this mode, individuals interrelate by pursuing mutually respected interests that they know conform to what is universal, reproducing an existing framework in which the universal serves as the means for realizing their particular ends on a par with one another. Due to this instrumental role, the universal in question is not particularized in itself, but only abstract, leaving the particular ends by which it is realized to be determined by personal discretion. The universal thus comprises more a set of general conditions to be upheld in conduct than a set of particular ends to be realized.[4] Markets entail this mode of interaction by bringing individuals to adapt their preferences and activities so that in satisfying their needs they satisfy those of others, duly respecting each other's property entitlements[5] while otherwise ignoring all further privileges that might differentiate their treatment of one another. In this manner, market participants conform to the universal network of economic interdependence in order to realize the particular ends that they pursue on an equal footing with others as individual commodity owners and as guardians of the livelihood of their own household.

Granted that commodity relations realize such willing, wherein the recognition of property and household right is universally observed as a condition for satisfying personal interest, why must law rest upon it conceptually, let alone in reality? In part, the answer is that a genuine legal system cannot operate unless individuals conceive the form of universality in objects and direct their will in regard to one another according to a universal,[6] instead of interacting in terms of particular factors that set them in different ranks with separate privileges. Legality requires that law be known and willed, and this requirement implies that the form of universality informs the particular ends and actions of individuals, enabling them to interact as equal subjects before the law. Legality does so not on the basis of shared values and agreement about substantive ends, for this would render law a purely instrumental rule, relative to particular groups. Legality rather brings its universality to conduct in terms of a mode of ethical community grounded in the common recognition of universal protocols for fulfilling whatever end a person chooses to pursue.[7] Such an association has a scope as universal as that of civil society and applies to all individuals interacting in recognition of their capacity as bearers of a self-selected interest on a par with that of others.

Even if this congruence is so, however, why cannot law be conceived and actualized on the basis of property relations and morality alone, in line with liberal theory, or in virtue of household relations, as praxis theory might suggest? In terms of the analysis of property rights and morality, owners already seem to know and will the general features of their property entitlements, just as moral agents appear to know and will the universal dimension of each other's right and welfare. In each case, disposing over property involves recognizing the ownership of others, just as morality always involves acting in a morally accountable way with respect to others who are held to equivalent standards. Similarly, the family binds its members in terms of a common good at whose maintenance they are obliged to aim.

Nonetheless, the administration of law cannot follow directly from property rights because property entitlements, taken on their own, have an entirely accidental existence, in that the mere strictures for giving one's freedom recognized existence in an external factor leave undetermined what will be the particular limits of each item of property. That this limitation leaves property claims without an objective, universal standing is made expressly evident by the modes of nonmalicious and malicious wrong endemic to the relations of persons.[8] Similarly, although moral subjects may concern themselves with the lawfulness of their willing, their activity does not conform to a universal that has objective existence insofar as they aim at a good that is an ought, awaiting realization through their personal initiative. The family, as a structure of ethical community, may situate its adult members within an existing common weal whose perpetuation they know and will, but this shared end lacks the form of universality both by being restricted to the particular household and by existing in the form of feeling.[9]

In the market, by contrast, where upholding right becomes an external compulsion for all in order to satisfy their particular interests, individuals engage in knowing and willing a universal that is both sufficiently abstract and sufficiently objective to make legality more than a paper writ. Insofar as it is known and willed by market agents, the universal in question is not the economic law realized in market activity behind the backs of the commodity owners who seek satisfaction for their needs by accommodating those of others. This universal rather resides in the recognized property entitlements of commodity owners. It is suitably abstract in that it is instrumentally affirmed by all market participants no matter what their intentions and wants, and it applies throughout the network of market relations, whose own economic law leaves to the personal discretion of commodity owners how to satisfy their market needs. This universal is suitably objective insofar as each market transaction is predicated upon recognizing the commodity ownerships of its respective participants, as well as those already at hand in the existing commercial relations that all must heed in choosing how to satisfy their needs. On both counts, market activity engenders a general observance of property rights, preempting any alternate arrangements where individuals relate as unequals, whose different stations in the community are governed by separate sets of rules relative to factors independent of their will. In this way, the market provides the type of economic conduct that allows legality to be realized.[10] If, instead, the economic roles of individuals are determined independently of their free choice of need and occupation by such factors as kinship, race, gender, caste, estate, or religion, then the universality and equality of law will run up against an incommensurable barrier.

Consequently, a systematic conception of ethics cannot follow the liberal route of advancing from property right directly to legality.[11] A family and a civil society organized as associations of freedom must first be conceived and realized before the household and social presuppositions for thinking or actualizing legality are at hand. Without a free family, in which spouses are equal partners in a marriage of their choosing, irrespective of natural differences, the household conditions for equal treatment under the law are just as lacking as are the social prerequisites for legal standing in the absence of a civil society, minimally involving a market in which individuals interact on a par in respect of self-selected needs for the commodities of one another. In either case, alternate institutions would prevail in which the privileging of factors given independently of freedom would obstruct the universality of legality.

It must be understood, however, that this service of a free family and commodity relations does not create legality on its own, for neither household nor market activity carries with it a positing of law or the enforcement of law by legal institutions. Marx, for one, misunderstands this truth when he suggests, albeit without argument, that commodity relations give rise to property relations and to legality.[12] It is patently absurd to argue that property arises from market activity, since commodity relations only proceed between individuals who acknowledge one another as owners of the goods that they exchange. However, if commodity relations cannot precede property since they incorporate an actual recognition of ownership, they can precede legality since they contain neither any legal stipulation nor any legal enforcement of this recognition. To precede, however, is one thing, to generate, another. Markets alone provide no resource for engendering legality. Law is not a matter of commerce, which the market can spawn as one more field of business.

The conceptual priority of commodity relations instead suggests that legality cannot abstract from property relations, moral subjectivity, family right, or the institutions of economic autonomy, both because these practices can operate on their own without relying on legal institutions and because individuals whose rights are upheld cannot participate in legal institutions without already enjoying the freedoms of market participation together with the personhood, moral autonomy, and family membership that economic self-determination encompasses.

Although legality can certainly protect the property, moral, family, and economic rights of individuals, each of these rights can be exercised whenever individuals choose to determine their own actions in consonance with the corresponding actions of their counterparts. Owners can respect each other's property without appeal to the law, just as individuals can hold each other morally accountable without bringing one another to court. Similarly, family members can honor their respective rights and duties as spouses, parents and children without legal intervention, just as market activity can continue even when legal authority breaks down.

Moreover, if individuals are deprived of their rights as persons, moral subjects, family members, or economic agents, they can hardly enjoy the status of a legal agent and freely avail themselves of the law. Deprived of property rights, individuals are tantamount to slaves, devoid of any independent legal standing. Deprived of moral accountability, individuals cannot be held legally responsible for their deeds or competent to stand trial. And stripped of family or economic rights, individuals are subject to the arbitrary will of household masters and economic oppressors, leaving them unable to affirm their rights through the law. Consequently, only when traditional family and social formations have been overturned, freeing household and community of bonds based in naturally conditioned factors of gender, kin, caste, estate, and the like, can law order the relations of individuals as free and equal legal subjects without contradicting their roles in family and society.

One might be tempted to conclude that legality rests upon the achievement of equal political freedom as well, following Marx's observation in *On the Jewish Question* that the rise of a democratic republic out of feudal society occurs concurrently through the same abolition of estate privilege engendering a civil society of independent individuals whose pursuit of private interest is regulated by law rather than birthright.[13] However, even if the democratic revolution is a "bourgeois" revolution in this sense of simultaneously giving birth to a free republic and a civil society, the equal treatment by law in civil society need neither apply to nor presuppose equal political participation. Although political democracy may not be realizable without a civil society in which social privilege is overcome, the participants in civil society need not be political equals. On the one hand, the members of civil society may not all be citizens of the same state, even though they all stand equal before the law as it applies to their property, household, and social affairs. On the other hand, fellow citizens may well exercise their property, moral, household, economic, and legal freedoms without participating in a properly constituted democracy. Political self-determination is neither included in nor a prerequisite for the exercise of civil rights, even if only a democratic state can uphold all spheres of right as a self-ordered system. Hence, legality does not presuppose political freedom, which is one more reason why legal relations are to be conceived in civil society prior to the conception of the state.

It might still be objected that legality must presuppose that legal subjects already exercise their political rights as self-governing citizens insofar as the origin and authority of law seems to reside in the political realities of its conformity with the constitution and in its proper enactment by the constitutionally specified legislature. However, as suggested above, legality can apply to civilians who do not enjoy political rights, such as aliens, just as the positing of law need not involve the acts of a legislature, nor reference to a political constitution.[14] Indeed, that the state requires law for its own operation only reaffirms how legality must be conceived prior to the conception of political institutions, even if legality, like all other prepolitical institutions, ends up being reshaped in view of the requirements of self-government.

Whereas reference to politics is thus premature, the way in which property, moral, household, and social freedoms do underlie law becomes manifest when the minimal character of legality is clarified.

The Minimal Determination of Legality

The determination of legality begins with the introduction of law itself, understood as nothing more than the positing of right in the form of public rules addressed to the knowing and willing of all members of civil society. This specification comes first inasmuch as any further determination of the specific content of law or of the machinery by which it is enforced must incorporate what is here at stake. No particular aspect of law can be conceived or realized without involving what is generic to law any more than any aspect of legal process can operate apart from law in general. Yet, minimal as it may be, the determination of law as the positing of right in the form of norms aimed at civilians is ambiguous and arbitrary unless the identity of "right" and the nature of its "positing" are established.

The "right" and the "positing" allegedly ingredient in legality's minimal determination are by no means independent givens. Rather, the character ascribed to law's positedness bears directly upon the content of right posited by legality. This relationship is evident in the two extremes that have distinguished traditional interpretations of the positing at work in law.

On one side is the purely formal characterization where law's positing contributes nothing to the content of the right that is made law. According to this view, basic to the conception of natural law given a privileged place in the teleological praxis theories of Plato and Aristotle, the valid content of law is dictated by reason such that the willing of legislators, by which law is posited, merely actualizes the rational content of what is good, discovering rather than creating the content of what is legal. In this case, the validity of law resides in its rational content, which is dictated independently of its positing. To the degree that this positing is wholly formal, what is posited is entirely rational, deriving all its legitimacy from the rationality of its content rather than from how and by whom it has been willed into being.

At the other extreme, there is the voluntarist characterization, figuring so prominently in Hobbes, where the positing of law is the source of both its content and authority. In this case, what counts as the right made legal is simply whatever the sovereign wills in positing law. Since here the positing of law is constitutive of legality's content and validity, the right realized in law is opaque to reason and entirely derivative of will. These extremes by no means exhaust the conceptions of law of their historical advocates. Just as Aristotle complements natural law with positive legislation whose content cannot be specified by reason but is merely local, changing and hence conventional in character,[15] so Hobbes restricts the content of what the sovereign wills into law by the imperatives of personal survival and liberty as antecedently defined in the state of nature.[16] Nevertheless, these extremes frame the range of possibilities from which we can choose.

Given how legality is situated within civil society, it might appear that the positing of law will have the same formality exhibited in the legislation of natural law in teleological ethics. For if legality is a structure of civil society, intelligible prior to political relations, yet posterior to the rights ingredient in property relations, morality, the family, and markets, then the positing of law cannot involve the act of legislation by political authority, whereas the content of law will be parasitic upon rights determined independently of legality. It would thus appear that the posited character of law will contribute nothing to its content and simply realize rights dictated by reason as embodied in nonlegal yet prepolitical structures of interaction.[17]

Nevertheless, this situation does not reduce the positivity of law to a merely formal character, nor does it leave the right posited in law identical in content to the freedoms at work in prelegal affairs. Even though the positing of law minimally ingredient in legality does not here depend upon the political institution of legislative enactment, it does contribute something of its own to the rights it posits, transfiguring their prior entitlements in making them legal.

These preliminary claims await their full substantiation. Granted that they be entertained, in what can the positing of law then reside and how does this positing affect the rights it legalizes? Above all, why should law first be conceived in this halfway house between the formal enactment of rationally prescribed rules and the pure positivity of a voluntarist legislator?

To approach these issues, it is necessary to keep in view the three stages by which legality ends up being progressively determined. First, there is law per se, understood as the positing of right or right as it attains the form of law without further qualification. Second, there is the determinate being of law, or law as it enters existence for the will and awareness of legal subjects. Last, there is the court of law, law as it is actually known and willed as a universal power and authority.[18] This ordering reflects how the court cannot be thought or realized without reference to determinate law, just as the particular existence of law cannot be determined without involving what is generic to law. We have, therefore, little choice but to begin with the account of law in general, considering the positing of right in and of itself without reference to the particularities of specific laws or to the operations of the court.

4 · Law as the Promulgation of Right

Right as Law

Granted the exclusive normativity of self-determination and the corollary that law must be conceived within the context of right, how is legality to be understood given that law has its first foothold within civil society, there standing minimally determined as the positing of right? To begin with, what is right as law? Is it nothing more than positive right in general?[1]

In one respect, positive right signifies the achieved correspondence of right and existence in the only way possible, through the actual willing of right.[2] For if right is normative conduct, which, given the identity of self-determination and validity, is the respected exercise of freedom, the existence of right cannot be achieved by natural necessity or accident but only by autonomous willing. Yet, then, to take one prominent civil affair, the actual willing of right would already be operative in commodity relations without any express rule of non-economic juridical law.[3] After all, whenever individuals exercise their economic freedom in market transactions, they therein recognize one another's respective commodity ownership and needs without having to appeal to any legal process. And willing right independently of law can just as readily be found in every property relation, moral engagement, and family affair that proceeds in recognition of the entitlements and duties constituting its respective mode of self-determination.

More, however, is required for right to be posited in conformity with its concept. Right must not only be an object for the will and consciousness of individuals but be present in a recognizable form appropriate to its character. Since right bears unconditioned validity, the only adequate form is universality, the element of thought, which alone transcends the limited, local, and relative character of anything particular. Hence, right that is posited as such requires an objective existence for agents in general that is determined through thought.[4]

Moreover, to attain an objective existence right must not only become given as an object for the consciousness of legal subjects, but it must also actually count as valid in the activity of individuals who interact in recognition of its authority.[5] If right only obtains the "object-likeness" of being known by legal subjects, in distinction from the objectivity of being universally realized in practice,[6] the exercise of freedom it represents remains purely ideal, a mere imperative awaiting realization. Yet, since the realization of right occurs through willing, which is always liable to the deviations of arbitrariness, the objectivity actualizing right cannot consist in a legality in which rectitude is automatic. Rather, law's positing of right must involve an enforcement of law that remedies the transgressions of right that now violate legal rules made knowable to all relevant rational agents. In virtue of this enforcement, making right both known to all in standing universal determinations and objectively actualized in function of this knowledge, law renders right something known as universally counting as well.[7]

The Objectivity and Universality in Law's Positing of Right

How law involves these dual dimensions of positing, of objectivity and of universal determination through thought, is basic as much to legal reality as to the conception of law.

Indeed, law, understood formally merely as a recognized public rule, can have the most arbitrary contents and still be "objective" either as knowable to all to whom it applies or as generally enforced. By the same token, law can be "universal" simply by mandating a type of conduct to some generally defined audience, no matter what it prescribes and prohibits. Nevertheless, insofar as normativity resides in the reality of freedom and that reality calls for legality, law will have legitimacy to the degree that what it posits is in accord with right.[8]

Consequently, valid law, which is the sole concern of normative legal philosophy, constitutively gives right an objective existence by publicly stipulating what counts as right, addressing in principle all agents to whom the rights in question apply. Such content is wedded to the basic form law has as the positing of right. Nonetheless, valid law's public stipulation of right does not guarantee that the law actually becomes known by all, for this ultimately depends upon the cooperative attention and cultivation of each agent, which publicity alone cannot effect, even when law is taught as a mandatory part of public education. However, if valid legal promulgation cannot posit right in the consciousness of all, it does posit it for consciousness in general, presenting right in a form that is at least knowable by all duly educated[9] legal subjects.[10]

In so doing, law achieves a basic requirement of right that sets obedience to law apart from conformity to laws of nature.[11] Since right consists in the recognized freedom to which agents are entitled, its actualization requires that it be made known so that agents can honor the rights of others and have their own entitlements respected in turn. Law provides this primary element in the realization of freedom, that right be made an object of knowledge to all who exercise the correlative rights and duties by which self-determination can proceed. The rule of law is not a matter of compelling individuals to conform to right in the way in which gravity compels objects to fall. As a positing of right, law can only realize entitled freedom by enabling individuals to know what rights they have and what obligations they thereby owe their peers.

Further, beyond making right generally knowable in an authoritative way, law makes right count in an objective fashion, rectifying the infractions of subjective behavior through the workings of the legal system. These workings are part of the efficacy of law, without which law becomes an empty writ. Yet these workings are equally dependent upon the promulgation of right as law, which first supplies the legal process with rules to enforce and adjudicate. Consequently, the objectivity right achieves simply by being publicly stipulated as law must be treated prior to the further objectivity right obtains through the legal process, whose conception ineluctably presupposes right in the form of promulgated law. This conceptual primacy holds even though legality shows itself to be a structure of ethical community where, accordingly, legality's constitutive rights and duties apply only within an existing framework of functioning legal institutions, whose operation involves a sufficient level of recognition to guarantee the efficacy of law.

Although the realization of right through the courts is conceptually subsequent to the objectivity law brings to right through its mere positing of public rules, that positing simultaneously determines right through thought, giving it a conceptual objectivity it otherwise lacks. Law involves this other dimension by mandating right in the form of a promulgated general norm, specifying right in its universality, as it applies in all relevant types of situations to all relevant types of actions and to all relevant types of agents. In each case, what makes types of situations, actions, and agents "relevant" to legal determination is their connection to the exercise of the rights that law posits. The content of legal rules will thus be parasitic upon the content of the rights it renders objective and universally determinate.

Language and Law's Positing of Right

To make right an object of consciousness and to determine right by thought, law must employ language, which alone can provide the medium for a prosaic public expression capable of capturing the universality of thought determinations. Simply articulating rules in speech is not enough, however, to effect law's positing of right.

First of all, the linguistic expression of law must be generally available to all legal subjects, not only by being in a language known to them but by using expressions and conceptions with which they are or can be made familiar through available resources. Otherwise law's articulation in language lacks the universal objectivity to knowing[12] required for right's adequate realization.

Moreover, the expression in language of law must be recognizable as the authoritative positing of right by those to whom it applies.[13] Otherwise, the commonly knowable writ of law is simply a list of rules with no practical relation to the wills of its audience.

With legal language both generally accessible and recognizably authoritative, the correlative features of publicity and universality that speech can convey enable law to bring right to exist in accord with its true form, that of a universal determination of the will enjoying objectivity.[14] Needless to say, the imperative to insure the accessibility and authoritative recognizability of legal promulgation bears upon how law is concretely determined in relation to the particular content of the rights it posits, as well as upon how legal knowledge is publicly provided and how legal process applies and enforces law.

The Nonpolitical Positivity of Law and the Recognition of Legal Authority

Significantly, whatever particular efforts are required to enable law to give right an existence conforming to its true form, this achievement in no way depends upon the political institution of a legislature or the other political structures by which constitutionality bears upon law. If it did, and political authority extends no further than the boundaries of self-rule, law could not apply to noncitizens and could never exist as common law or international law. What permits law to be positive yet accommodate all these examples is that law's minimal positing of right simply pertains to the public promulgation of norms, something that gives right an objective existence with a universal content whether the law in question exists as a matter of common law or statute. On this score, it is perfectly appropriate for legality to be conceived prior to the conception of the state.

Conversely, the fact that law's positing of right need not involve legislative enactment signifies that law cannot initially be defined as the will of a sovereign. Although imperatives of political self-determination may entail that law ultimately be sanctioned by the legislative act of a duly elected legislature, this stricture does not preclude that legality has a character given independently of self-government, a character that may well be a prerequisite for valid political association.

Within the confines of civil society, however, how can law carry the requisite stamp of authority? Must appeal be made to political institutions and the ultimate sanction of constitutional fiat, conferring authority upon a legislative or judicial source of law? In that case, of course, law could not be conceived prior to the state, raising all the foregoing problems that plague efforts to determine law as a purely political affair. Alternately, does the authority of law rest upon an appeal to a basic norm or rule of recognition,[15] acknowledgment of which entails embracing standards for recognizing rules as valid laws?

This route opens the possibility of conceiving law within civil society, provided that recognition of a basic norm or its equivalent can occur without transcending civil association.

But is any such appeal to a basic norm or primary rules really necessary, especially prior to an account of constitutionality, which may be essential to valid political institutions but which may hardly be a prerequisite for legality in its civil dimension? After all, any basic norms or primary rules are themselves laws whose authority must be recognized. Yet precisely because they are basic, they cannot have their authority conferred upon them through recognition of any further rule or legitimating factor. Hence, recognition of their authority is direct and self-sufficient. But then, why cannot law itself count as law by having the same direct and self-sufficient recognition, where law has its authority precisely in being recognized as the public universal positing of right? Such recognition of law as immediately authoritative allows legal rules to count without appeal to any further norms or institutions and thereby escape all the attendant problems and superfluous repetitions that recourse to foundations involves. Accordingly, the authority of law can be recognized in such a way that legality can proceed within civil society wholly apart from any constitutional groundings. However these groundings may necessarily apply when self-government presides over law and all other institutions of right, they play no determining role in the prior civil dimension of legality.

Law's Transformation of the Content of the Right It Posits

The fact, however, that political legislation is not constitutive of the promulgation of law does not entail that the positing of right effected by law is merely formal, leaving what is legal something determined entirely prior to the positing by which right becomes law. On the contrary, the objectivity and universality right attains in becoming law bears upon its content in several important ways.

Posited in the form of law, right gains existence as something whose realization is predicated upon it being known in principle to all to whom it applies and being known to them in terms of its universal specification as a general norm applying to types of conduct. As such, the content of right is liberated from the hold of feeling, passion, self-seeking, opinion, and the form of revenge that burdens it as long as it is defined in terms of the resources at hand in the interaction of property owners, moral subjects, family members, and market agents.[16] Whereas these interactions all leave the boundary of their respective rights subject to conflicts and violations they cannot authoritatively resolve alone, law gives right an objective content, whose application to particular cases may be subject to dispute but whose provisions are at least given in common for all, enjoying legal validity precisely in being posited in this recognizable and recognized form. Consequently, insofar as valid law posits every right that is susceptible of external regulation,[17] the making legal of each such right adds to its content the feature of being authoritatively stipulated and recognized, that is, being legally valid.[18]

Moreover, in order for right to enjoy a determinate legal recognizability, law must promulgate sufficiently uniform and specific qualifications for identifying the particular entitlements of individuals so that the exact extent of their rights can be authoritatively proven.[19] Unless law prescribes feasibly determinate standards for what count as valid deeds, contracts, marriages, adoptions, and so on, the boundaries of property, family, and economic entitlements remain plagued by the same ambiguities that the legal promulgation of right is designed to overcome.

The Normative Superiority of Law over Custom

By itself, the objectivity provided by law's positing might still appear to alter the content of right in only one respect, that it now be qualified as what has been proclaimed a valid rule of conduct for all. This qualification would leave right posited as law little different from right that is alive in custom and habit. For in distinction from the blind conformity to law achieved by instinct in animals, what is done from custom is certainly known by those who follow it.[20] However, what does distinguish customary right from law proper is that the content of custom is not stipulated for all in an authoritative common form. Instead, it is something individuals come to know in a subjective and accidental manner, according to their particular lived experience and the specific examples of customary behavior they may encounter. Hence, the content of custom suffers from an indeterminacy that betrays the universality of specification by thought.[21]

Even for a scientific observer, as opposed to a participant in customary practice, determining what custom is can only be discovered by observing examples of its behavior and by extrapolating about what patterns actually prevail in the community at large. These claims can never be more than the pragmatically conditioned generalities of any empirical investigation. Indeed, the difficulty of ascertaining the content of prevailing custom is precisely what has often led to the supplanting of custom by legal promulgation. Such was explicitly the case with Charles VII's 1454 Ordonnance de Montils-les-Tours, which resolved the problem of indeterminacy by authoritatively recording custom, transforming it into a body of written law. This innovation, however, saddled the legal system with the local scope of custom, setting the stage for replacing the resulting patchwork of regional laws with a unitary law of the realm.[22]

These problems of indeterminacy of content and locality of reach are compounded by the special problem custom poses as a measure of valid conduct. For customary "law" leaves ill-defined how what ought to be done is to be distinguished from what happens to be done.[23] Since custom consists in whatever pattern of observances prevails, every deviation from putative custom may just as well be the rule of a new custom if it be sufficiently followed. Furthermore, given the indeterminacy in encountering current custom, distinguishing what is deviant from what is permissible is all the more problematic. Implicitly observed in outer behavior and inner sentiment, rather than explicitly recognized in posited rules, custom cannot sustain any firm contrast between factual regularity and normative practice, habit and duty, or making and obeying rules.[24] On all these counts, custom cannot be a satisfactory vehicle for the realization of right.

Right posited as law, by contrast, has a content ordered by thinking and publicly knowable by all, thereby exhibiting the objectivity and universality appropriate to right. This quality might be considered a mark of deficiency as against custom's reality as something at hand in the life of the community. Yet law's promulgation of right as a universal content in no way precludes this content from being any less present in the conduct of individuals.[25] Not only may valid laws remain enshrined in custom even after they are publicly promulgated,[26] but individuals may abide by law just as much or more than they abide by custom. Indeed, what law allows is that the content of right not be present solely in existing practice but be at hand in a form by which it can be objectively known by all and realized on the basis of their common knowledge.

Contrary to Plato's suggestion in the *Republic*[27] and to much traditional practice in the East,[28] a community does not reveal itself to be more just simply because it dispenses with law and employs training and custom to lead its members to conform voluntarily to unpromulgated patterns of harmonious conduct. Such sacrifice of legality at the altar of paideia and custom not only fails to guarantee any greater conformity with norms of conduct but insures that those norms lack the objective and rational determination that law's positing of right can alone afford.

Of key significance for the legitimacy of legality is this elementary feature of law's positivity: far from simply undergoing a change of form, right that has been made law is rendered distinctly different in content from all rules to which individuals can conform independently of knowing of their public promulgation. Whereas such rules can be followed in practice in the way in which matter passively receives form, only known laws can be truly obeyed out of duty, where obedience involves self-determination on the part of the agent.[29]

This exclusive truth of obeying legally promulgated rules holds strictly even in respect to action in conscious obedience to the edicts of moral accountability and conscience's determination of good purposes and motives. Admittedly, to paraphrase Kant's apt formulation, moral action is conduct undertaken not just in conformity with law but in function of a conception of moral principle. Nevertheless, the inability of moral subjectivity to achieve objectively recognized determinations of good conduct and overcome disparities between different consciences leaves morality unable to provide any unambiguous fulfillment of duty. As a structure of ethical community falling within civil society, publicly stipulated law can overcome the ambiguities of moral reflection by providing an authoritative positing of right whose obligatory character rests upon an antecedent recognition of legal authority. In this fashion, legality can alone give right the duly objective and universal determination comprising its true content. Given the normativity of freedom, duty can consist in nothing but the observance of right. Consequently, individuals can act for the sake of observing right in its truly determined content, that is, obey law out of duty, solely when custom gives way to legality and legality complements the freedoms of property relations, moral reflection, family life, and the market.

Dilemmas of Conflating Law's Positing of Right with Judicial Precedent

Similarly, it makes little sense to treat law in general as if it could lie in the decisions of courts, whose judicial precedents serve as a customary body of legal standards. Such a collapse of law's positing of right with judicial behavior may well reflect the genuine concern that without an established pattern of court behavior, laws lose all objectivity and universality in the face of the utter caprice with which judges might otherwise apply legal rules. Yet such a justification for recognizing judicial precedent presupposes the independent objective and universal determination of law, without which the courts have neither any law to interpret and apply, nor any legal standing of their own as privileged judges of cases.

Moreover, if judicial precedent is treated as the determiner of what law posits as right, right loses the very objectivity and universal determination that the appeal to court tradition seeks to redeem. What counts as judicial precedent is just as much hostage to the vagaries of experience as the boundaries of custom. Judicial precedent cannot be established unless judges have the authority to determine independently what the law means and unless a pattern of judgment equally arises that can be referred back to earlier court decisions. Yet even determining whether past decisions fit earlier decisions, enabling the latter to serve as a precedent in the first place, falls within the prerogatives of judicial interpretation, which can always change.[30] Consequently, not only is the identity of judicial precedent deprived of an authoritative objective and universal determination, but judges cannot help being just as much constrained as unconstrained by any pattern of decisions they might acknowledge.[31]

On this sorry basis of case "law," determining what is legal becomes an aimless, indeterminate quest with no real beginning or end. Reduced to judicial precedent, legality forfeits its objectivity and universality, turning into a rule of custom in which distinctions between rule-making and rule-following or between prevailing behavior and normative conduct can no longer be sustained.[32]

Law as the Positing of Right in Its Truth

By positing right in a form both universal and objective, thus overcoming the indeterminacies of custom and rule by judicial precedent, law can well be said to provide right with its true determination.[33] In the first place, since right, the respected existence of self-determination, is the very formula of valid conduct, its content is both universal and objective. Its content is universal because right is not relative to any particular circumstances. Right's identity with the recognized reality of self-determination is precisely wherein lies its freedom from foundations, a freedom that, in positive terms, gives itself its own determinacy and thereby exhibits the self-grounding character allowing for universal validity. By the same token, the content of right is objective insofar as it is determined independently of any reference to a particular subject.

In order for right to exist in a form corresponding to its content, that is, in order for right to have an actuality in accord with its concept and thereby exist in its truth, the reality of right must be both universal and objective. Law, as the positing of right, comprises just such a realization.[34]

As we have seen, law's public promulgation of right sets it in a form that is universal in two respects: making right legal realizes right in the form of rules that are themselves universal in content, prescribing a general type of conduct for legal subjects in general; and these rules are addressed to all legal subjects, making their universal specification of right something available to every relevant agent in exactly the same way.

In virtue of these two aspects of universality, law gives right an existence that is objective, once again in two correlative respects. Right posited as law is rendered objective in the sense of being made an object of the knowledge of all agents falling under its scope, and right thereby achieves an objective existence in that law gives right a unitary authoritative determination independent of the different experiences and perspective of individual legal subjects.

Consequently, law that posits right permits right to gain a truthful existence to the degree that the actuality of right corresponds to its concept. Without legality, the rights of persons, moral subjects, family members, and market agents remain caught in a predicament fraught with contingency and conflicting interpretations, leaving the specification and realization of their respective entitled freedoms bereft of any universal and objective determination.

The Limits of Reason in the Positivity of Law

Does this then mean that law gives right a reality that is determined by reason in a thoroughgoing way? Valid law, as an element of civil society, will be rationally determined to the degree that it posits in the form of publicly recognized rules the entitled freedoms that the concepts of property rights, morality, the free family, and civil association themselves dictate. Yet, even though each of these spheres of right has its own prelegal character, determinable by the reason of systematic ethics, legality's transformation of these rights into promulgated rules adds something to their respective content that involves more than simply the recognized universality and objectivity of legal form. Each law has a definite specification, which, even if it is not a decree commanding particular individuals to perform particular acts in a particular situation, still must come to a unique determination concerning such matters as amounts of compensation and punishment. Although further aspects of this specification fall properly within the account of the particular determination of law, which incorporates and presupposes the concept of law in general as the positing of right, law must still involve details that cannot be decided by reason alone, even if these details are nothing more than the legal formulation of the principles of right.

This overdetermination has its root in the relations of right as they are given antecedent to any legalization. In their own exercise, property rights, moral self-determination, family entitlements, and equal economic opportunity themselves involve dimensions of discretion where the specification of the actual boundaries of particular entitlements, of their violations, and of the righting of these wrongs goes beyond reason, independently of the positivity that law brings into play. Property relations set the stage by engaging two dimensions where discretion cannot fail to enter: in deciding the purely quantitative dimension of violations of right and the corresponding amounts of compensation or punishment and in the qualitative measuring required when the exchange value equivalence of different types of factors must be assessed.[35] Since property rights are component prerequisites of every further exercise of freedom, these dual sources of overdetermination continue to apply in every instance where the external aspects of household and economic rights must be legally defined.[36] This observation holds true, despite the appearance that laws mandating so-called indeterminate sentencing might be able to overcome such positivity. Although such laws may specify a range of punishment within which courts are empowered to make the final decision, this range has its own specific boundaries, which are just as opaque to strict rational deduction as any "determinate" sentence.[37] Consequently, just as when law is not at hand, persons, moral subjects, family members, and civilians must decide the specific dimensions of particular entitlements without any strict guidance from reason, so legality must add its own authoritative decisions when it posits right as publicly promulgated rules.

Of course, no matter what particular content is assigned specific laws, each one retains a universality by prescribing realizations of right and rightings of wrongs for types of conduct involving types of agents and types of situations. Since conduct is always individual, however, involving unique agents pursuing unique courses of action in unique situations, the application of law cannot be wholly governed by further laws, allowing for a mechanical implementation whereby machines could supplant interpretive judgment with their rote operations.[38] This divide between the universality of legal rules and the individuality of conduct, which is endemic to law, thus already sets the stage for a legal procedure in which an authoritative judgment is made to decide how law should be applied to individual cases. The positivity of law as the public proclamation of right thus entails a further positivity, consisting in the exercise of discretion that cannot be expunged from the application of law. On both counts, reason may specify the boundaries within which discretion is exercised but not the particular outcome that gets decided. Hence it is just as wrong to claim that reason can wholly determine the publicly promulgated content of law[39] as it is to insist that law can be applied by reason alone.

The Global Dimension of Civil Society and Law's Positing of Right

A further aspect of the nonpolitical character of law's positing of right reflects the global dimension of civil society.[40] The rights of civil society are no more limited by national boundaries than are the market institutions through which they have their immediate expression. Consequently, the challenge to enforce equal social opportunity is international in scope, permitting and indeed requiring global regulations of market activity that should apply to citizens and noncitizens alike, within and without national territories.[41] Similarly, since the property, family, and economic rights operative in civil society have a universal extension, independent of membership in a particular body politic, law that posits these rights, whether eventually statutory or not, enjoys in principle a universality and objectivity of equally international jurisdiction. As history testifies, this universal scope may well set very practical limits upon what individual national legislatures are able to enact in face of existing international arrangements.[42] Consequently, the publicity of law is no more necessarily restricted to a national audience than judicial processes are exclusively limited to national courts. By the same token, when law in civil society operates within a particular state, legal authority extends to citizens and noncitizens alike.

For these reasons, the conception of legality within civil society does not involve any distinctions between domestic and international law. Such distinctions cannot, of course, be systematically drawn until the just state and its relations to other states have been conceived. Consequently, what holds normatively of law in civil society will apply to law in the state as well as to law in the community of nations.

5 · The Form and Content of Law in Civil Society

The Systematic Problem of Determining What Form and Content Law Should Have

Law has its minimal normative determination as the positing of right, situated within civil society and stipulating those of its members' rights susceptible of an external regulation. Such positing consists in the generally accessible and recognizably authoritative public proclamation of rules specifying how to exercise the enforceable rights to which members of civil society are entitled and how to right infringements of those entitlements. This prescriptive determination of law is basic insofar as it presupposes no other features of legitimate legality, whereas all further aspects of valid law incorporate it.

What, however, follows conceptually from this normative determination of law in general? Must any account of the particular form and content of laws and of the legal process that applies them to individual cases appeal to the facts of legal history, thereby forfeiting all prescriptive ambitions in deference to describing how law becomes historically concretized? Or does the concept of right provide the resources for mandating the particular form and content that law must have to be normatively valid? If ethics were a formal discipline, allowing for an independent legal philosophy of equal formality, the only option would be describing the historical phenomena of law. Yet, since ethics establishes the normativity of self-determination as a self-ordered system of institutions of freedom, the prescriptive concept of law need not be aborted at its most abstract specification.

If reason is to prescribe what particular form and content law should have on the basis of law's general normative determination as the positing of right in civil society, all that can be drawn upon are the structures of freedom of property relations, morality, the family, and civil society. Otherwise, the concretization of law would be undermined in one of two ways. If factors given independently of the workings of self-determination were relied upon to specify law, legality would be infected by heteronomous elements, devoid of any authority to mandate what law should be in particular. If, alternately, law was concretized through factors of freedom from spheres of right beyond civil society, such as the political arena, law would be defined by terms for which a systematic account has yet to be made. Although such terms may well entail further bodies of law, such as those regulating political activity and government, paying them their due heed must await the conception of the body politic.

How, then, can law obtain a particular determination mandated by how right is realized in civil society? The prescriptive concept of law in general and the concepts of property, the family, and the institutions of economic freedom provide all that is needed. Although moral freedom is incorporated in civil society, it cannot factor in determining law's particular content. Because law is posited as a rule external to each rational agent and applied to each by other participants in legal association, it cannot regulate the internal self-legislation of moral autonomy or any other essentially internal matter, such as love or feeling. Law can command only what can be obeyed in an external performance.[1] Accordingly, since valid law in general is nothing but the positing of right in civil society, law obtains its proper particular form and content in function of how the principles of the three externally enforceable spheres of freedom in civil society, property relations, the family, and the just economy, get translated into publicly promulgated law.

The Particular Content of Law in Civil Society

Since legalizable right in civil society consists in a system of property, household, and economic entitlements, law becomes validly concretized as a system of legal rules giving an objective and universal determination to the rights of each of these three domains. Accordingly, the system of law in civil society will divide itself into three basic branches: property law, family law, and economic law. Moreover, each branch will be subdivided in accord with the fundamental features of its respective institutions of freedom, as they are constitutively organized and correspondingly grasped by reason in the preceding parts of the philosophy of right.

The Basic Divisions of Property Law

The legalization of property rights comes first conceptually insofar as property entitlements presuppose no other rights and are incorporated in all other forms of freedom. As with every other division of law, property law must stipulate its respective rights so that they are clothed in legally defined formalities that allow for legal proof and adjudication.[2] Otherwise, law fails in its endeavor to give right an objective and universal determination.

Property law first will provide legal regulation for the property entitlement presupposed by all others, the inalienable ownership by each person of his, her, or its[3] own body. This provision involves not only offering legal certification to the immediate physical embodiment of each person but proscribing all forms of enslavement and other undeserved violence to the body of individuals.

It also entails giving legal guarantee to the right of necessity (*Notrecht*).[4] The right of necessity comprises the entitlement of each individual to enjoy the physical and psychological preconditions of personhood, even when this requires partial, particular impositions upon the property of others. Such partial impositions upon others' property rights deserve legal sanction insofar as they uphold the very survival of a person, without threatening the entire personhood of any other property owner. If this condition is met, the impositions upon property rights are justified insofar as they serve nothing other than the very realization of these same rights. However, if individuals committing a particular wrong out of necessity may escape criminal responsibility, their victims are still due compensation for the harm they have suffered, and it is a public responsibility to insure that such compensation is provided.

The right of necessity has as its inverse counterpart the "good Samaritan" duty of individuals to aid others in peril provided rescue depends specially upon the personal intervention of that potential good Samaritan, the latter knows or should know these features of the situation, and such aid does not endanger the rescuer. Property law must draw the boundaries of this duty, which constrict the more public aid is provided individuals in function of the right of necessity. For every advance in legally enforcing the right of necessity diminishes the occasions for good Samaritan relief. In addition, property law must specify the limits of care by which individuals must abide to avoid engaging in the negligent conduct of knowingly putting other persons in unreasonable risk of mortal jeopardy.

With the inalienable domain of each person legally demarcated and secured in these ways, the law of property will next be in a position to specify the rules concerning taking ownership of external factors that are not already the property of another person. Although civil society may well already incorporate virtually all ownable external factors under respected bonds of commodity ownership, making contract the predominant form of property acquisition,[5] this development does not render superfluous this area of property law. Even in the context of a full-blown civil society, there is still room for taking ownership of external factors that are not already the property of another, whether on the periphery of markets or in their midst when factors devoid of previous relation to economic need become objects of market demand. The latter include the labor power of individuals, of which individuals take ownership by legally designating a limited portion of their activity as a means of earning.

Having specified how persons legally appropriate alienable property, property law will be able to stipulate the legal rules pertaining to the maintenance and use of one's own property. Although this issue will subsequently be qualified by the imperatives of family and economic rights, property law will have to lay down its own rules in support of the rights of persons to use their property and not have their person or property jeopardized by other owners' use of their belongings. This effort will involve that portion of nuisance law that prohibits owners from using property in ways that undermine the property rights of others, without yet taking into account the impact of use upon economic welfare and other entitled opportunities deriving from the further spheres of the family, civil society, and, eventually, the state.

On this basis, property law will next specify how persons may alienate their alienable property, either by abandoning it or transferring ownership to another person. Since the transfer of ownership requires the agreement of both giver and receiver, property law will stipulate a body of contract law, which will fall into two major divisions, corresponding to the two basic ways in which property may be transferred: the law of gift contract (where one person gives the title or partial use of property to another without recompense) and the law of exchange contract (where the title or partial use of property is traded). Property law will here specify what constitutes sufficient knowledge and independence to enter into contractual agreements in good faith, doing so with respect to the requirements for exercising one's rights as an owner. Further considerations relating to the wider claims of family and economic rights may well qualify when contracts are duly convened. Nevertheless, property law itself is restricted to drawing its own specific guidelines solely on the basis of how individuals determine themselves as owners.

In this regard, since property rights, like all other rights, can be violated nonmaliciously or maliciously, and malicious wrongs can be done either through fraud, negligence, or unconcealed coercion, property law must stipulate the appropriate legal modalities for righting these different forms of wrong. On the one hand, property law will mandate how nonmalicious wrongs are righted. Since such wrongs do not involve any criminal volition, punishment is not at issue. Instead, property law must stipulate how injuries and damages are to be assessed and how victims are to be compensated. In the cases where nonmalicious property losses can be retrieved in kind, the law will mandate restitution of the property together with compensation for any further related losses incurred by the victim or gains received by the malefactor. In cases where damage and injury does not allow for restitution of the original state of affairs, compensation will be mandated according to some specification of the value of the injury and losses suffered.

Whereas property relations themselves provide no measure for such value other than in the equivalencies agreed to in particular contracts, the context of civil society provides another measure, of particular importance for equal economic opportunity: the market value of commodities, including labor power. Since law posits right in civil society, it is in a position to employ the market's determination of price, income, and rent in assessing compensation, as well as in determining when contractual agreements lead to unfair gain and loss that call for either canceling or modifying their enforcement. Within the framework of property law, however, determinations of unfair gain and loss pertain only to discrepancies between market prices and the represen- tation of the values of goods and services in contract. Further consid- erations of distributive justice depend upon family and economic right, which impinge upon contract within the edicts of family and eco- nomic law. However this qualification occurs, since law provides for a public and authoritative determination of property entitlements, it must also mandate how compensation will be provided in cases where nonmalicious perpetrators do not have sufficient resources to com- pensate their victims. Otherwise the property rights of the victim will remain wronged.

The proviso that nonmalicious perpetrators are responsible for res- tituting the due property of another that they have used or taken in good faith follows directly from the structure of nonmalicious wrong. Since nonmalicious malefactors have appropriated what is not theirs, the right of ownership clearly mandates that they relinquish that prop- erty or its equivalent to its proper owner. In such cases of nonmalicious wrong, liability can be said to be strict, since fault does not figure as a requirement for providing compensation.

On the other hand, responsibility for compensation in the case of non-negligent accidental damages or injury might appear unfounded on property relations alone. In this case, the nonmalicious malefactor may well have caused damages or injury or been responsible for prop- erty that occasions such losses. Yet, since the nonmalicious malefactor has not purposely willed what occurred, either directly or indirectly through negligence, should that agent still be held liable for damage or injury? And if not, is the law required to mandate compensation for the victim at public expense? Victims of accidents may be entitled to have their person and property respected, but can an accident any more than a purely natural disaster count as a wrong whose righting is obligatory? Is liability strict for either the "precipitators" of unintended loss or the public?

Indeed, on the basis of property relations alone it may seem doubt- ful that persons can be held liable for injuries and damages suffered through non-negligent accidents to which they are connected, either bodily or through their alienable property. Not only is malicious voli- tion absent, but the precipitator of the wrong is not in illegitimate possession of any property that can be restituted, as in cases of con- flicting property claims.[6]

However, as we have seen,[7] property right makes owners liable for compensating any harm caused accidentally by or on their property, whatever their purposes and intentions may be. The moral distinction between act and deed, limiting moral responsibility only to what is done on purpose and what consequences are intended, is of no import in nonmalicious wrongs. The factors to which accidental harm are tied are not merely things in relation to moral agents but property embodying the will of an owner, irrespective of that person's ends and welfare. As a consequence, as long as the victim has not suffered harm in the course of trespass, the owner is liable for compensation but not deserving of punishment. As the positing of right, legality must promulgate the limits of such liability and determine how it will be enforced. In addition, the law must specify how victims will receive compensation at public expense when liable owners are unable to meet their responsibilities.

Moreover, if law is to uphold the person and property of individuals, it must mandate giving what each is due, even when damages and injuries to the entitled objectivity of persons results from accidents or natural events for which no other particular owners are liable. Consequently, property relations do make it a public responsibility to maintain personhood and the external domain by which it has its objective freedom against the ravages of so-called "acts of God."[8] In these cases, right requires that the limits of tort liability be supplemented by a publicly administered accident insurance. The same imperative will apply where, owing to the expense, delays, and uncertainties of tort litigation itself,[9] the rights of victims can only be met through public provision of compensation.

As we have seen, property law must also similarly stipulate everything that might fall under the right of necessity (*Notrecht*),[10] which sanctions particular infringements upon property entitlements when necessary to maintain the survival of persons. This obligation to provide for the preconditions of personhood does not extend as far as the wider economic right to the conventional standard of living making economic independence possible, a right left to economic law to posit. Nevertheless, legalizing the right of necessity does involve publicly guaranteeing the physical and psychological survival needs of every person. Moreover, in the context of civil society, when legality sanctions particular infringements of property in order to sustain the personhood of another, any individual loss that is not commonly born is itself deserving of public compensation. In all cases, since it is the public, not specific individuals, who are targeted as liable to provide for these necessities of personhood, the equality of right is upheld.

When, however, particular property entitlements are not violated for the sake of survival, property law must stipulate punishment, as is due for crimes violating the person and property of individuals. Restitution cannot be substituted for punishment because crimes in civil society are malicious wrongs, involving not just harm to the legal rights of specific individuals but violation of right in general as it is posited by law. Therefore, criminals must be held as felons deserving punishment; they cannot be treated as civil offenders, whose only responsibility is to provide due restitution or compensation.[11] Any approach to "corrective justice" that follows Aristotle in ignoring this qualitative difference in how nonmalicious and malicious wrongs should be balanced out[12] treats crime with impunity, sacrificing the very fabric of law for an exchange of costs.

Indeed, because the distinction between nonmalicious and malicious wrong lies not in harm to the rights of others but in a malefactor's willing against right in general, criminal attempts can count as crimes even when no one's entitlements are infringed upon, just as there can be victimless crimes completely undirected to harming others.[13] In the context of civil society, where prepolitical freedoms are the substance of normativity, victimless crimes would have to amount to acts that are proscribed by law because they undermine the autonomy of the agent even if they do no harm to others.

Whatever the case, given the normativity of freedom, the only ground for punishment is the guilt of having willed explicitly against right, which in the case of property law is the right of owners to the security of their person and property. Rehabilitation cannot be the rationale for punishment, since that implies that the criminal is in need of tutelage to become capable of doing right, and, therefore, that the malefactor was not fully responsible for the "crime" and thus not a bona fide criminal. Instead of deserving punishment, the malefactor would be in need of instruction or treatment.[14] Any notions of parole that reduce punishment based upon judgments of how far a criminal has been rehabilitated during incarceration suffer from the same incoherence.[15] Similarly, law itself must not be understood as a tutelary instrument for making legal subjects better. Any such notion, so prominent in ancient teleological ethics and in the legal systems of

Communist regimes,[16] presupposes the lack of full autonomy on the part of legal subjects and is therefore antithetical to the normativity of freedom and the corollary determination of law as the positing of right.

Deterrence cannot be the reason for punishing criminals, either. Punishment for the sake of deterrence would allow for punishing innocent individuals in cases where they could be made to appear to be guilty as a lesson to others. Moreover, by exclusively privileging the psychological effect of the punishment upon future behavior, whether of that individual or others, deterrence punishment would disrespect the right of the criminal to be held responsible for his or her act.[17]

Nevertheless, because law posits right in civil society, the meting out of punishment ought not be indifferent to its social ramifications. Property right mandates that the punishment fit the crime insofar as the criminal's volition against right can only be measured according to the degree to which the crime violates the personhood of others and the degree to which that violation was committed with malicious premeditation. Yet since right is now posited by law in civil society, the criminal's volition against right is here a volition against the law as it governs and upholds civil society. Now, if crime goes unpunished, it is law whose validity is challenged.[18] Consequently, the severity of the wrong involves not just the injury to the crime victim but the injury the crime signifies to the legal fabric of civil society. Accordingly, the punishment must also fit this ramification for civil society, which will vary depending upon the strength of the social order and the corresponding social harm that the crime represents.[19] Although the wrong of crime thereby acquires an added dimension, the very efficacy of legality may well lessen the significance of the injury to right in general and entail an easing of the punishment.[20] Since the stipulation of penalties will thereby be relative to the situation of civil society, so will that part of the legal code comprising its penal laws.[21]

The need to punish the criminal in order to uphold legality's enforcement of right admits considerations of deterrence, not regarding whom to punish but in determining the amount of punishment.[22] In this way, the preeminence of guilt as a basis for punishment remains respected in due recognition of the freedom of the criminal.

Whatever the case, since the victims of crime also suffer injury, loss, and/or damage to what is legitimately theirs, a suffering whose magnitude is not altered by the relative strength of the legal order, property law must not only punish malefactors but also compensate their victims. Here, the law will incorporate the different approaches compensation must take according to whether restitution is possible in kind or only in value and whether such compensation can be provided by the malefactor or must be provided by public means. Needless to say, any legal system that does not guarantee compensation for victims of non-malicious as well as malicious wrongs is unjust.

The Basic Divisions of Family Law

The structures of family freedom similarly provide the principle for differentiating family law. Insofar as the family involves, on the one hand, a relation between spouses, who may or may not have children, and, on the other hand, a relation between parent/s and children, family law will analogously divide its legal stipulations to cover the rights and duties of spouses to one another and the rights and duties of parent and child.

Regarding the juridical relation of spouses, family law must first of all specify the requirements and modalities of marriage, whereby individuals become spouses. The law must stipulate a particular procedure or procedures that qualify as recognizable marriage agreements and insure that the requirements for marriage accord with the rights of family membership. While specifying what qualifies one as a consenting adult, the law must equally mandate that no extraneous factors, such as gender, sexual orientation, race, religion, nationality, caste or other hereditary ranks, or the permission of other parties restrict the free choice of adults to marry one another.

Having legally defined the requirements and procedures for entering marriage, family law must then stipulate the rights and duties of spouses to one another. Since spouses are the juridical partners of a single private domain situated beside other families and single persons, the law must regulate spouses' relations both to one another within the household and as representatives of their family in civil society. In each sphere, family law must give legal formulation to the equal right of spouses to share in making household decisions as they pertain both to affairs within the family and to affairs relating the family to other individuals and institutions. In addition, family law must stipulate the responsibilities of spouses to provide equal care for each other's welfare. Even though spouses may have property of their own, excluded by prenuptial agreements from being consolidated within the joint private domain established by their marriage, the prerogatives of joint management of household affairs and joint concern for their common welfare make the use and disposal of property a chief concern of family law. Consequently, as much as family law presupposes property law, it must qualify property relations where necessary to uphold the specific rights of spouses.

Finally, family law must stipulate under what conditions and by what procedures marriages can be abrogated. Once more the law must provide an objective and universal formulation that heeds the responsibilities of spouses to one another regarding comanagement of the family property and care for one another. This provision includes the incorporation of laws of estates to the extent that inheritance affects a surviving spouse's claims on the household property.

The relation of parent and child, which may or may not involve relations of spouses to one another, similarly mandates the divisions of family law that posit its different rights and duties. To begin with, family law must stipulate the requirements that qualify an adult to be the juridical parent of a child. The relation of parent and child is not biological; it is a normative relationship involving a recognizable committed responsibility on the part of the parent to provide for the child's development to autonomous maturity. Accordingly, the law must specify the conditions under which individuals are the accountable parents of their offspring and when individuals qualify as the parents of children who are not their biological progeny. These conditions should not involve gender, sexual orientation, race, caste, nationality, religious affiliation, or any other factor not constitutively linked to an adult's ability to raise a child conscientiously to maturity.

Family law must thereupon stipulate the rights and duties of parents as guardians of their children. Since the legitimating standard for parental authority is here providing children with the means for becoming autonomous individuals, able upon maturity to exercise their rights as persons, moral subjects, independent family members, and participants in civil society,[23] family law must specify what this requires. The law must also specify what procedures must be followed when parents are derelict in their care, whether nonmaliciously or with malice. In this connection, the law must stipulate what privileges parents should enjoy as guardians over their children. The law must also stipulate how all these rights and duties are to be shared by spouses, who, according to the freedom and equality of the marriage relation, should be treated as equally responsible guardians of their children. These responsibilities must further be defined in view of divorce and remarriage, both with respect to previous children and new additions from prior marriages of one's spouse. In this light, family law must also stipulate the rights of children to inherit property in the name of their parents.

In addition, family law must determine the responsibilities parents owe to children who are born out of wedlock, be they their own biological offspring or that of their spouse. To the degree that the biological parents of a child are responsible for that birth, they are juridically accountable for the welfare of the child, whether they are married or not, until other adults have legally adopted the child. Consequently, "illegitimacy" does not of itself disqualify a child from the right to obtain from the duly responsible parents adequate support and a fair inheritance. Finally, family law must specify when children qualify as adults and leave the guardianship of parents.

Since, in each case, the rights and duties posited by family law can be violated nonmaliciously or with malice, legal remedies must be provided for both varieties of wrong. When spouses fail to honor their duties to one another nonmaliciously, the law must stipulate how the exercise of freedom that is infringed upon is to be reinstated, together with compensation for any resulting losses. Similarly, when parents nonmaliciously fail to fulfill their responsibilities as guardians of their children's welfare, the law must mandate how their children are to have their welfare upheld, whether through supervision of parental behavior or a new adoption, as well as how they are to be compensated for any damages incurred at the hands of parental neglect. Conversely, family law must stipulate how children who disobey and flee the due authority of parents are to be brought back under parental control. Although children may intentionally violate the prerogatives of parental supervision, their status as minors leaves their infraction a matter of nonmalicious wrong, for which punishment is inapplicable.

However, when competent adult family members maliciously violate their duties as spouses or parents, family law must stipulate both the compensation due the victim and the punishment due the malefactor. This provision complements the property law that already applies to spouses in their capacity as persons, entitling them to be free of bodily coercion and to dispose freely over whatever property has been set apart as their own through prenuptial agreement. Now, the law of the family has the obligation to stipulate that individuals who intentionally refuse to give their spouses an equal role in household affairs or fail to care for their common welfare are just as liable to punishment as are parents who maliciously neglect their children.

Since spouses are, in principle, partners in the common private domain of the family, holding one responsible for compensation for injuries and losses suffered by the other only applies either in reference to separate properties underwritten by prenuptial agreements or to property separations that follow upon divorce or marital annulment. However, when, in either case, the malefactor is unable to provide due compensation to the victim, the law must stipulate how compensation is to be publicly provided.

The same principle applies to cases of malicious parental neglect. Since children of such parents have a claim to the family property as it applies to their upbringing, any additional compensation they are due should either be withdrawn from other parts of the family property or from property set aside through prenuptial agreements or following upon divorce. Once more, when the malefactors are unable to provide due compensation, family law must specify the modalities for publicly obtaining what is owed the victim. Analogously, family law must stipulate how to provide adequate care to children at public expense when parents are unable to do so owing to circumstances unrelated to any malice or negligence on their part.

Finally, insofar as every free agent enjoys the rights of family association in conjunction with being obliged to respect those of others, family law should have its own "good Samaritan" provisions mandating that individuals at least notify legal authorities when they witness violations of the rights of spouses, parents, or children.

The Basic Divisions of Economic Law

Economic law, for its part, is obliged to give legal form to all the rights by which economic autonomy secures its reality. The broad divisions under which this task is fulfilled are once again determined by the concept of the corresponding structures of freedom. Broadly speaking, economic right revolves around realizing the equal economic opportunity that enables individuals to satisfy self-selected needs for commodities through occupations of their own choosing in reciprocity with others.[24] The institutions by which economic right has its actuality involve three dimensions of civil society: the market, economic interest groups that jointly advance their members' shared economic welfare, and the public administration of welfare that overcomes the inability of markets or economic interest groups to ensure by themselves the economic equal opportunity of all.[25] Accordingly, economic law will be differentiated in function of these three structural domains of economic right.

What could be called market law will specify the modalities by which individuals are entitled to buy, trade, and rent commodities (including labor power and capital), the legitimate rules pertaining to employment and the production process, and the organization of enterprises, whether public or family-owned, worker self-managed, or share-issuing corporations. In so doing, market law will, in the first instance, promulgate how the entitlements already specified in property and family law are to be sustained within the concrete setting of economic relations, where individuals interact not simply as persons and family members but as individuals satisfying their self-selected needs for commodities through interdependent earning activities. On the one hand, this promulgation will involve specifying the formalities by which property ownership and contractual obligations are made to count in commercial transactions. In all cases, market law must ensure, in conformity with property rights themselves, that no factors extraneous to the relevant acts of will (such as gender, sexual orientation, race, nationality, religion, caste, kinship, or age differences among capable adults) be allowed to restrict who may participate in such transactions or how they may do so. On the other hand, market law will be obliged to mandate how trade and production must proceed so as not to undermine the freedoms of persons and family members. In this respect, market law must insure the personal health and safety of participants in economic affairs, as well as prevent commerce from despoiling their property and guarantee that engagement in market activity not prevent individuals from fulfilling their duties as spouses and parents. Conversely, market law must insure that economic affairs be regulated so that family members are not economically disadvantaged due to meeting their obligations to care for children or spouses in need.

However, because market law promulgates the universal and objective determination of economic freedom, it imposes its own modifications upon property and family law in behalf of the demands of equal economic opportunity. In this respect, Unger is wrong to identify the regime of contract with the market.[26] Just as not all property can take the commodity form (each person's body being the prime exception) even if all commodities are property, so not every freedom of contract can enter into the freedom of commodity exchange. Economic right requires that contractual freedom be molded to promote economic justice so that, for instance, as Unger himself acknowledges,[27] unfair transactions are not enforced and market price does enter into determinations of due compensation.

However, even if market law stipulates laws whose enforcement attends to these imperatives, the possibilities of economic disadvantage are not removed. The law of the market may well protect the commodity ownership and family integrity of individuals, prohibit discrimination or household obligations from prejudicing their entry into commercial transactions, and set its own limits to what comprise enforceable contracts. Yet the very operations of market activity will still give rise to inequalities of wealth, disparities between supply and demand, and unequal development of the common infrastructures of economic activity so as to interfere with the exercise of equal economic opportunity that needs markets for its realization.[28]

Insofar as market agents have the right to try to overcome this predicament by banding together into groups to promote the particular economic interests they share, economic law must extend to stipulating the valid modalities of these corporate activities. They have an internal and an external dimension. The former pertains to the internal organization and membership policies of economic interest groups, whereas the latter pertains to their action towards other economic agents, whether individuals or other economic interest groups. Economic law must promulgate rules to ensure that membership in economic interest groups is open to all individuals sharing the interest in question, irrespective of any extraneous factors, such as differences of gender, race, religion, sexual orientation, kinship, hereditary rank, or age. Moreover, economic law must mandate rules holding economic interest groups accountable to their members. Economic law must also regulate the relation of economic interest groups to one another and to unorganized economic agents, ensuring that such groups advance their respective common interest without violating the economic rights of others.

Nonetheless, no matter how rigorously market law enforces the valid options of economic interest group activity and no matter how forcefully individuals take advantage of their opportunity to make common cause to advance their shared interests, equal economic opportunity remains unguaranteed. Because every economic interest group remains dependent upon other independent market agents to satisfy their needs, no group can be sure of succeeding in promoting its own interests, nor is there any guarantee that the success of one group will not leave other groups and unorganized individuals in a weakened economic position.[29] Consequently, the legalization of economic interest group activity still leaves economic law with an abiding challenge: to make legal the public regulation of market activity devoted to achieving equal economic opportunity.

This remaining sphere of economic law mandates a public administration of welfare, which, broadly speaking, must enforce rules overcoming the two complementary barriers to the realization of economic freedom.[30] On the one hand, economic law must stipulate rules guaranteeing individuals the marketable commodities to earn a living of their choosing in reciprocity with others. This guarantee involves insuring that all economic agents have sufficient resources, whether capital, adequately trained labor power, or other saleable or rentable commodities, not to mention the general education, health, sustenance, and shelter required to engage in market activity allowing them to satisfy self-selected needs. On the other hand, economic law must mandate rules insuring that sufficient amounts of affordable commodities are produced and brought to market to satisfy the needs of individuals, as well as that the market provide enough earning activities to allow individuals to obtain through freely chosen occupations the commodities that they choose to need. In conjunction with these dual imperatives, economic law must insure that commodities are not only affordable but safe and safely produced and that earning activities proceed so as not to undermine the physical and psychological preconditions for exercising economic freedom. In addition, when individuals are unable to exercise economic independence because of mental or physical hindrances, economic law must provide for their welfare on a par with others.

In order to achieve all of these aspects of the realization of economic freedom, economic law must always obey the proviso of restricting particular market activities only in order to advance the general exercise of economic self-determination. Consequently, wherever possible, laws directing production or redistributing wealth should employ instruments of monetary taxation so as to leave economic agents as much choice as possible in deciding what goods to trade and what services to render. If economic law instead relies upon public doles of specific commodities or unilateral assignments to particular occupations, the battle to overcome economic disadvantage will only restrict the economic freedom it should be making generally available.

Because all such measures must cope with the given economic conjuncture, which is itself always prey to external influences as well as to the contingent course of market decisions, the actual public administration of welfare must continually revise its strategies in face of changing conditions. Nevertheless, the imperatives of economic freedom give economic law basic mandates that no market developments can ever supersede. It is these imperatives that give this final section of economic law its abiding differentiation.

Needless to say, since the exercise of economic right upheld by economic law is just as tied to the duty of respecting other's right to enjoy the same opportunity, market agents should be subject to "good Samaritan" laws obliging them to seek aid for anyone they discover having their economic rights violated, provided furnishing such aid is specially dependent upon the personal initiative of those prospective good Samaritans and such intervention does not put them in jeopardy. Once again, the more economic law succeeds in enforcing economic right, the less occasion there will be for "good Samaritan" obligations to be in play.

Since economic law can be violated nonmaliciously or maliciously and, in the latter case, covertly or with brazen disregard for the economic rights of individuals, economic law can enforce those rights only insofar as it stipulates due compensation and due punishment in accord with the different infringements that are possible. As much as victims of any other form of wrong, victims of economic wrong deserve due compensation, whether or not the perpetrators are able to provide it themselves. Hence, economic law must mandate public provision for such compensation. Similarly, economic law must take into account the injury to the social fabric in stipulating punishments for economic crimes.

To the degree that the basic outlines of property, family, and economic law follow from the concept of right and the concept of law's positing of right in civil society, they have general features mandated by reason that are indispensable to the realization of justice. Admittedly, the actual laws within each division must stipulate particular rules that ineluctably involve positive elements opaque to reason. These specifications, which can only be determined by choice without any strict rational guidance, include the particular formalities constituting valid property deeds, contracts, marriage agreements, child custody, and the like, as well as specific punishments and compensations. Nevertheless, the rational core defining the central divisions of the content of law in civil society provides a body of principles suited for enshrinement in a constitution lording over positive legislation. Otherwise, the legal stipulation and enforcement of these principles is prey to the arbitrariness of legislators, depriving the positing of right of any firm commitments. However, since constitutionality and the relation between legislation and constitutional statute are matters inconceivable apart from the state, the issue of how the content of law has a constitutional element cannot be treated in the consideration of law in civil society prior to the conception of politics. What is clear, nonetheless, is that law in civil society is susceptible to, as well as in need of, a partial constitutional enactment.

The Form of Particular Laws in Civil Society: The Legal Code

Far from yielding the concretization of law to historical description, the philosophy of right is able to specify the particular content law should have in civil society by taking the externally enforceable dimensions of property right, family right, and economic right and conceiving how they get posited as law. What form should the resulting divisions of property, family, and economic law take? Is this question beyond philosophical dispute, leaving the matter to comparative studies of the forms laws have had and which institutions might be most compatible with certain historical structures?

If reason is to tackle the issue in a systematic fashion, it must once more restrict itself to the resources it has already put on the table. In this case, the philosophy of right has made available two crucial factors: the prescriptive concept of law in general and the concept of the particular content of law in civil society. These are sufficient to do the job, for what is at stake in determining what form particular laws should take in civil society is how to posit the differentiated content of law in a form satisfying the requirements set by the concept of law in general.

These requirements have been shown to involve general accessibility to and recognizable authority for all legal subjects. How must this be achieved, given the prescribed content of law in civil society?

The Rationale for the Codification of Law in Civil Society

To begin with, the same considerations still apply that precluded law's positing of right from having to be statutory. Given the global dimension of civil society, the particular content that law should have is by no means confined within national boundaries. Since property rights, family rights, and economic rights apply to agents irrespective of political differences such as the distinction of citizens and aliens, the law positing these rights may just as well be international as domestic in scope. On this account, such law may take the form of international treaty as readily as that of domestic legislation. By the same token, when such law is domestically enacted, nothing in the scope of the rights it stipulates prevents their legal promulgation from occurring as federal as opposed to merely state or provincial legislation.

For complementary reasons, the requirements of general accessibility and recognizable authority by no means depend upon statutory enactment. On the one hand, statutes may fail to be generally accessible or recognizably authoritative. They may be so voluminous, inchoate, or technical as to be beyond the comprehension of legal subjects, or they may count as empty writs, devoid of any binding character. On the other hand, the requirements of general accessibility and recognizable authority appear to be attainable without legislation, as the example of "common law" and nonlegislative codifications suggest.

The notion that the form of law in civil society need not be statutory is further buttressed by the fact, as cited above, that the rights of civil society have a global dimension that makes international treaty a fitting form for their legal positing. International conventions are not the product of bona fide legislation by an international sovereign, which would be a contradiction in terms.[31] They constitute a law of a different character, one that is no more the will of a sovereign than the decision of a legislature.

Yet if law in civil society need not be statutory, what must be true of its form to enable the law's particular content to be both generally accessible and recognizably authoritative? The indeterminacies and particularism afflicting custom render any customary form inadequate. This inadequacy applies as much to unwritten traditions of nonjudicial behavior as to traditions of judicial precedent, where the determination of law is relegated to particular judges' assurances of the authority of particular past decisions. As we have already seen, neither option provides a form for law that can confer general accessibility or recognizable authority upon any definite content. In both cases, what the law is remains relative to particular experiences of customary behavior and particular perspectives upon such experience. Moreover, the expanse of experience to be sifted through by one judicial authority or another disseminates into the endless stream of particular conduct and cases, where determining which past verdicts count as relevant precedents is left to the whim of each presiding judge, whose own verdict then generates a potential precedent of its own.[32] This predicament prevents legal subjects from having any manageable access to what the law is or any firm criteria by which to sanction any pattern of conduct, judicial or otherwise, as the emblem of an authoritative determination of the law.

What solves these problems is codification, understood as the systematic organization of the particular laws of civil society into a single body of rules, published in some form to which all legal subjects can have access. This codification may occur through legislative action, by independent scholarly effort, by the agreement of lawyers and judges, or by the fiat of conquerors. Indeed, codification may involve not making any new laws but simply rationally ordering those that are already at hand.[33] Whatever the case may be, two features render a legal code a form that enables the particular laws in civil society to be generally accessible and recognizably authoritative.

First, the code unites all rules that count as law into a recognizable single body, inclusion into which provides an unequivocal standard for knowing when a rule has legal validity. Thus, the particular laws of civil society have a recognizable authority provided the code is made public in a way that allows legal subjects to discover what rules fall within it. The second cardinal feature of codification, meanwhile, facilitates such discovery. Namely, by uniting all particular laws in a systematic fashion, the code provides a tool for obtaining knowledge of the law, no matter how voluminous it may become in face of the complexity of civil society. Although the body of law can hardly avoid becoming both too large and too technical to fall within the comprehension of any one individual, the principle that law is binding only for those who can have knowledge of it need not be made a mockery.[34] As long as the law is rationally codified in terms of the universal divisions of property, family, and economic rights,[35] the corresponding division of the legal code gives individuals a skeleton key for locating any specific law.

What guarantees the possibility of a systematically organized legal code is the systematic character of the concept of right. Insofar as each structure of freedom is determined in virtue of either incorporating less determinate interactions of right or by being ingredient in more encompassing institutions of freedom, the differentiation of rights has a completeness that allows a legal code to possess a definitive differentiation. Although changing circumstances can continually call for new laws, these laws will never explode the framework of the legal code, provided that its divisions are rooted in the different dimensions of property, family, and economic rights.[36] Each new law will simply fall under the heading of whatever exercise of right it involves. That each law will fit under some such heading is guaranteed by the prescription that law promulgate right.

The Dual Structure of the Legal Code

Accordingly, the legal code has an open texture that remains systematically organized. Each law will have positive aspects, whose determination cannot be decided solely by the concept of right. As we have seen, these positive elements involve such matters as the specification of punishments, compensations, and the formalities by which certain exercises of right are legally recognized. Consequently, simply by changing the positive element, new laws can always be added without transgressing any universal strictures of right. Because alterations in this positive dimension of law do not violate the principle of right it posits but only give it a particular realization, the legal code can retain an abiding scaffold capable of incorporating any valid law.

The legal code will therefore have a dual structure. On the one hand, the code will possess definitive universal differentiations corresponding to the basic divisions of the rights it stipulates, rights which in the first instance are those of property, family, and economic relations but later become supplemented by those of due process and political association.[37] On the other hand, the legal code encompasses the endless specializations of these areas.[38]

The completeness residing in the code's ability to incorporate all further elaborations within its fixed universal divisions is therefore not equivalent to the idle notion of a legal code in which every law and every feature of each law is derived from the principles of right. Such a legal code would be devoid of any positive dimension and therefore forfeit its very own status as a positing of right. Moreover, it would be incompatible with the structures of right, which themselves contain positive elements where, within certain limits, the reality of freedom is defined by will independently of reason. To demand that a legal code be beyond all elaboration is therefore futile.[39]

Requirements for Guaranteeing the Accessibility of the Legal Code

Granted the possibility and normative imperative of a systematic legal code, legal subjects must have it made available to them if it is to achieve its normative aims. This availability requires, first, affordable access to the code, whether published in print, electronic media, or some other instrument, and whether available in public facilities, such as libraries, broadcasting, telephone or other public access media, or for private purchase in books, compact disks, or on-line services.

Furthermore, the legal code must be formulated so as to be as accessible as possible to ordinary lay individuals. Not only must the legal code be promulgated in a language or languages intelligible to every legal subject, but the wording of laws must be stripped of any unnecessary jargon that impedes general understanding. Otherwise the law risks becoming the private preserve of a privileged group of legal experts, leaving everyone else at their mercy.[40]

Moreover, the formulations of the legal code must be framed within fixed, shared understandings sufficient to guarantee that its meaning will be reasonably unambiguous. Otherwise, individuals who have access to the words of the code and competence in the language of its expression will still be unable to comprehend with any certainty the putatively universal and objective law to which they are held accountable.

Nonetheless, access to the legal code remains without guarantee even if all legal subjects can know its words, speak its language, and reach common interpretations of its formulations. No such measures can prevent the complexity of property, family, and economic relations in civil society from engendering a mountain of equally byzantine laws. As a result, the legal code cannot avoid acquiring a technicality and girth that poses hurdles for any lay understanding. In the face of this problem, affordable legal experts must be made available to all legal subjects to enable them to know any aspect of the law they desire. Moreover, the legal expertise publicly guaranteed to all legal subjects must not be of inferior quality, a risk whenever legal aid takes the form of publicly employed lawyers whose experience, case load, support, and financial remuneration compares unfavorably with the private sector. In any event, however this service is equitably provided, whether through publicly provided legal insurance, personal legal cost allowances combined with public regulation of legal fees, or some other system, it is an intrinsic element of the due publicity of the legal code and distinct from the provision of affordable legal aid in going to court.

Since such publicly guaranteed help in understanding the law is necessary in order for the legal code to furnish law in a duly accessible and recognizably authoritative form, legal subjects have a right to it, a right that must itself be stipulated within the code. Moreover, since this right is indispensable to legal justice, it can be said, by way of anticipation, that it should be constitutionally guaranteed alongside the other rights of civil society. Consequently, a civil society that guarantees legal aid for its members only when they appear in court violates their legal right to have access to the law. The high proportion of legal practice that is devoted to advising clients prior to and apart from litigation is indicative of the significance of this right.

Interpreting the Legal Code

In order for right to be posited in civil society in a form adequate to its content, law must be promulgated as a legal code, providing general accessibility and recognizable authority. Yet how can the legal code be assured of giving right the universal and objective intelligibility it is supposed to command when every rule of the code can only be known by way of interpretation?

Ordinarily, this difficulty is considered in terms of the problem of judicial decision and the related issues of statutory construction and constitutional review. "Rule skepticism" presents the problem in a radical form by arguing that law has no fixed determination of its own but gains meaning only in function of how judges interpret it. Accordingly, as Justice Holmes would have us believe,[41] law is nothing but a prediction of judicial behavior. In that event, access to a common law will depend upon two coordinate endeavors. On the one hand, knowledge of case histories will have to be provided to legal subjects to give them a prudential basis for predicting future judicial decisions. On the other hand, judges will need to toe the line of judicial precedent, since otherwise, in the absence of any further necessitating principle, no predictions of future judicial behavior will be possible, leaving law a riot of arbitrary eruptions.

Yet can law be simply a plaything of judicial interpretation? How thus could judicial argument retain any meaning? Would not any justification of court decisions be reduced to the solipsistic exercise of judges predicting their own decisions? Moreover, as H .L. A. Hart has powerfully argued,[42] judges cannot even engage in authoritatively interpreting the law unless they are already subject to a commonly acknowledged law identifying who counts as a judge, what is the text of the law judges are to apply, and what procedures judges must follow in reaching decisions. All these matters are beyond interpretation to the degree that they must already have an unambiguous, generally recognized meaning if the legal system is to function at all. In this respect, law garners its fixed core of commonly shared meaning precisely from the fact that legality is a structure of ethical community, in which legal rights and duties only figure within an institutional framework already recognized to embody them.

Similar arguments have been offered by Dworkin with regard to statutory construction and constitutional review,[43] according to which the very possibility of engaging in interpretations of legislative and constitutional statute is the antecedent existence of a political community united in recognition of a political good already embodied in the institutions of constitutional self-government. Accordingly, statutory and constitutional interpretation always proceeds within a framework of shared principles, saving law from an anarchical dissemination of meaning.

These arguments have their place within the proper framework. Hart's refutation of "rule skepticism" duly falls within the consideration of the legal process of the court, and Dworkin's considerations belong within the conception of political institutions.

The problem of interpreting the legal code, however, cannot be systematically addressed by appealing to such arguments. No factors specific to the court or to legislation and constitutionality can be brought to bear. To do so would be tantamount to arguing in circles. The valid role of judge presupposes the reality of the legal code, whereas the political conventions of legislation and the constitution presuppose law in civil society to the degree that democratic self-government rests upon civil institutions. Conseqently, if the legal code is to possess a communicable common meaning for the members of the legal community, it must do so in virtue of the resources contained in civil society, independently of how these resources are further incorporated in the legal process and political association.

Contrary to the self-annulling specter of deconstruction, for which every meaning is textual and every text is at the play of its interpreter, a legal code, like any other significant convention, cannot be recognized for what it is without possessing a communicable meaning, for which variant interpretations must be peripheral. Since, normatively speaking, law in civil society posits right as it is first given in property, family, and economic relations, the legal code must translate those rights into standing laws with a universal and objective determination. To be subject to interpretation as such, the specific formulations of the legal code must first be recognized as codifications of right. This recognition stamps them with the commonly acknowledged meanings that individuals already respect in exercising their rights and honoring their duties in the interactions that constitute property relations, family association, and economic affairs. Hence, even without appealing to the legal process and political association, civil society contains law such that the legal code cannot even begin to operate without being recognized as a codification of common structures of freedom in which each responsible individual participates in his or her capacity as owner, family member, and market participant. Since one exercises one's rights only in function of honoring the rights of others, a basic shared understanding of their fundamental structure is unavoidable. The possibility of such common recognition is rooted in nothing more than the universal character of right and the universality of language and conceptual thought. Any attempt to deny this possibility founders in self-referential inconsistency.[44]

Although these considerations do not rule out all ambiguity, they do impose a context of shared understandings that limits how far the legal code can be alternately interpreted without calling into question the very framework that gives its rules their legal status. In this respect, legality is like every other sphere in which interpretation figures: interpretation can begin only on the basis of shared understandings unambiguously defining what is to be interpreted and how. Otherwise, there is nothing determinate to interpret and no determinate method with which to proceed. Only a discourse that surmounts all appeal to the given can overcome this doubly conditioned hermeneutic situation. Although systematic philosophy can aspire to have freed itself from hermeneutics, the positivity of the legal code stamps law with a residue of givenness that renders it an object of interpretation for all who are obliged to conform their conduct to its measure.

Ramifications of Codification for Legal Education

With law concretely determined in a legal code, legal education is freed from the forensic and pragmatic character it is forced to assume under common law, where legal expertise means knowing how to look up cases in law reports and legal practitioners can assume the role of familiarizing law students with the empirical investigation of judicial precedent.[45] Once law is codified and enjoys legitimacy as the positing of the rights of civil society, legal education can take a more academic and theoretical bent. Now knowledge of the law is to be sought not in case books but in treatises on the code and in philosophical treatments of property, family, and economic rights, as well as in discussions of legal procedures themselves. Accordingly, university teachers can supplant legal practitioners in legal education, just as academic works can

supersede judicial decisions as primary aids in discovering and interpreting the law.[46]

These transformations apply both to the education of legal experts
and to the general education in law to which all legal subjects are
entitled.

6 • The Legal Process

The Challenge of Enforcing the Legal Code

By promulgating a legal code to which all legal subjects are assured access, law gives right an objectivity and universality dictated by the requirements of right's own normativity. Although valid codification posits the rights of civil society in an authoritative form, however, the legal realization of right remains incomplete. The promulgation of the legal code may stipulate right in a form sufficient for the knowing of all legal subjects, but right will still not be actualized unless the laws are applied to individual cases of conduct in an objective and universally recognized manner. If the enforcement of the code is instead left to the vigilance of private individuals, the adjudication of alleged wrongs and the meting out of compensation and punishment remain subjective initiatives, prey to the resistance of others and liable to count as personal revenge entailing a new wrong of its own.

How, then, can law be enforced in an objective and universal fashion adequate to right? The same rationale that requires that right be promulgated as law mandates that whatever constitutes the authoritative way of enforcing law be itself legally specified. Otherwise, the valid enforcement of law remains entangled in the equivocal vagaries of custom and precedent, precluding any universal and objective determination. Consequently, whatever else it may turn out to be, the enforcement of law should be a self-realization of law, following its own legal strictures. In other words, the valid enforcement of law must be a legal process whereby law gives itself reality.[1]

Yet how should the legal process of enforcement be determined?

Systematically speaking, the only resources that can legitimately be drawn upon are the valid institutions of civil society and the legal code that seeks to uphold their constitutive rights. The problem, then, is to establish how the legal code should be enforced in the context of those civil institutions. The very predicament of conduct in property, family, and economic relations already testifies to how wrong can only be righted in an objectively binding manner by surmounting the limitations of merely personal acts and judgments. A public power must preside over the enforcement of law and do so so as to warrant the recognition of all legal subjects.

Given that the legal code need not be statutory, the public power that is required need not be politically defined as a branch of government enforcing the bills of the legislature. Otherwise, the account of legal process would have to fall within the concept of the state and await the determination of political institutions. Moreover, insofar as right in civil society has a global dimension, the legal process need not be limited to a national institution nor discriminate between citizens and noncitizens.

Nonetheless, granted that the legal process proceeds within civil society on a potentially global plane, can it be any further specified by reason? Is there a valid legal process in general with features constitutive of any legitimate enforcement of law and thereby susceptible of a purely conceptual account? Or are there many legal processes without any common dominator? Or is the specification of the legal process a matter of history, bound by culturally given predilections for one style of enforcement over another?

Admittedly, property, family, and economic law, the different branches of law in civil society, raise the possibility that a different legal process might be required for each. Moreover, the distinction between the different kinds of wrong, namely, of nonmalicious wrong and of open crime and fraud, might well entail differentiations between civil and criminal procedures. Further, the obdurateness of the controversy between the so-called "inquisitorial" and "adversary" trial systems raises the possibility that reason offers no clear justification for one over the other and that perhaps the legal process does not have any necessary normative core.

Nevertheless, none of these factors preclude reason from prescribing what the legal process should be in general. For even if the different spheres of law and/or the different types of wrong call for particular legal procedures of their own, each may still exhibit common features that permit them all to count as valid enforcements of law. Further, the disparity between "inquisitorial" and "advocacy" trial systems by no means rules out the possibility that both share in what is generic to a valid legal process or that only one may enjoy that honor and warrant exclusive adoption.

Since the resources at hand to decide the issue consist in the legal code and the framework of civil society, the question is whether these prescribe any determinate form to the legal process regardless of what sphere of law is at stake, what kind of wrong must be righted, and whether or not "inquisitorial" or "advocacy" styles are to be embraced. By contrast, the manner in which judges and courts have come into existence is a historical issue entirely distinct from the normative problem of determining what character they should have.[2]

Universal Features of the Legal Process

The very concept of a legal code stipulating the rights of members of civil society entails that a legal process enforce that code. Since right has unconditioned validity, it is imperative that it be realized in the form appropriate to its own objectivity and universality. The right and duty of public authority to bring the legal code to bear upon conduct in a legal fashion can therefore not be predicated upon the subjective willingness of individuals to submit to its jurisdiction.[3] If the legal process cannot be conditioned upon consent, however, as liberal reveries would have us believe, how is it otherwise determined?

Because the legal code consists in rules specifying a type of situation, a type of sanctioned conduct, and the compensation and penalties that are due victims and malefactors in cases of the corresponding type of wrong, the legal process must mediate between the generality of these prescriptions and the individuality of actual cases of conduct. This mediation involves four successive stages, reflecting the four steps potentially awaiting every application of law to individual cases.

The first stage, logically, occurs when a case is brought before the law. In the second stage, the relevant facts of the case are authoritatively determined so as to provide a duly proven state of affairs to which the law can be applied. Third, the recognized facts of the case are subsumed under the law in an authoritative judgment, whose verdict is legally binding. When a verdict is reached requiring compensation, punishment, or compensation and punishment, this judgment must be succeeded, fourth, by a legally stipulated and publicly enforced execution of the sentence.

The second and third stages are the constitutive affairs of the court, that public institution of the legal process receiving cases brought before the law for adjudication and remedy. The first stage, which accordingly comprises the legal process bringing cases to court, falls to the hands of public powers such as public registrars, grand juries, and police. The fourth and final stage in which compensation is secured and punishment is executed falls to public collection agencies and penal institutions.

Because all of these stages are constitutive aspects of the enforcement of the rights that law stipulates, their processes are themselves governed by law. This law, whose body of rules of legal enforcement must now be incorporated in the legal code, stipulates the specifically legal right of individuals to have their property, family, and economic entitlements legally enforced by having violations of one's rights brought to court, duly adjudicated, and duly remedied through punishment and/or compensation.

Bringing a Case to Court

To start with, individual cases must be brought before the law in a legally stipulated manner by a duly recognized public authority. A personal initiative may well set in motion this step, playing a role that may vary according to whether the wrong is nonmalicious or criminal. Nevertheless, the opportunity to bring a case to court must be publicly guaranteed, together with whatever resources are necessary to make this opportunity a reality. Without that guarantee, access to the legal process remains in doubt, depriving individuals of the secured opportunity to have their rights protected by law. It makes no difference what branch of law is involved, nor whether the wrong is nonmalicious or criminal. The right to legal protection of one's external freedoms extends to all without exception.

Moreover, because right in civil society is stipulated in a legal code, upholding right is now tantamount to upholding the rule of law. Righting wrong is therefore no longer a matter of an injured party alone but equally a matter of an injury to legality. This ramification holds true as much in cases of nonmalicious wrong as in cases of crime, for in each, legally protected rights are in need of enforcement. Consequently, the public authority enforcing the law has its own stake in taking ultimate responsibility for bringing all legally defined wrongs before the court.[4]

Since implementing law consists in upholding a right of one or more individuals in face of an alleged wrong committed by someone else, each legal process must bring before the law the likely parties to the case. Insofar as the enforcement of right requires this first step, these parties have both a legally guaranteed right to come before the law and a legally binding duty to do so when upholding the rights of others depends upon it.[5] Once more right and duty go together, for unless others are obliged to appear in court when the enforcement of my rights requires their legal cooperation, my right is violated, just as theirs is trampled if I observe no duty to cooperate with their court proceedings.

The right to have one's case come before the law is hollow, however, if the right and duty of court appearance is impeded by obstacles rooted in inequalities of wealth, education, health, or any other factors that should not bar the carriage of justice. Just as the legal code must be accessible to those to whom it applies, so the process of bringing a case before the law must be both within the means and within the understanding of the parties involved.[6] Whatever legal formalities are involved must be made intelligible and available to all concerned, whether through education or the provision of qualified legal experts. Moreover, all prospective cases must be accorded whatever preliminary investigation is required to frame them for legal consideration. Otherwise, individuals will be unable to have their case brought before the law owing to ignorance or need. Consequently, when legal subjects do not have the resources to inform themselves of and to engage in the legal procedures for bringing their case to court or to carry out whatever preparatory findings are required, these must be provided at public expense, without prejudice to quality or quantity. Since these measures are all aspects of legal subjects' right to have their entitled freedoms be protected by the law, they must be stipulated in that additional section of the legal code prescribing the authoritative procedures of the legal process.

Because the bringing of a case before the law is distinct from applying the law to that case, the public power that facilitates this step can be kept distinct from the public authority that subsumes the case under the law. Indeed, allocating these different stages of the legal process to different public bodies is imperative. Such a division of powers within the legal process not only takes advantage of the technical benefits to be had from specialized expertise but, more important, prevents conflicts of interest from arising where the authorities responsible for initiating a legal proceeding may be more concerned with vindicating their indictment than seeing right served.[7]

Needless to say, whatever measures are taken by the properly circumscribed public authority to bring a case before the law must conform with the rights of legal subjects. This requirement does not mean that public authority is powerless to impose upon the property prerogatives, family activities, and economic affairs of individuals in order to engage them in this or any further step of the legal process. Individuals should be compelled to come before the law when required by the enforcement of right. Since the bringing of indictments cannot ordinarily rest upon facts that have already been investigated in court, it can only base itself upon likelihoods,[8] where the chance of proving the facts of the case in court is at least possible. Consequently, these likelihoods are sufficient to oblige suspects to appear in court.

However, this compulsion cannot legitimately involve jeopardizing their health, property, family welfare, or economic independence. Legal authorities have an obligation to provide for compensation or the provision of care when engaging in the legal formalities of bringing cases to court prevents individuals from enjoying their rights and fulfilling their correlative duties as owner, spouse, parent, or economic agent.

The Public Character of the Court and Trial Publicity

To activate the law and legally enforce the rights of persons in civil society, public courts must be constituted to consider all individual cases of wrong that require adjudication and remedy.[9] Courts must be public in two respects. First, courts must be public bodies, for only then can they count as more than particular private powers and command universal recognition as the exclusive authority for judging cases and delivering binding verdicts. Accordingly, it is a public responsibility to provide for their expenses and to furnish enough courts with sufficient staff to enforce the law expeditiously. A civil society that tolerates inordinate backlogs in court proceedings does its members an injustice.

Second, court proceedings must be public. Because the legal promulgation of right properly involves codification of the law, the rationale for the publicity of court proceedings cannot be based upon appeals to imperatives of common law. The openness of court proceedings is not required because it is the only way the public can know what judges decide and through this mediation discover the judicial precedent determining what the law actually mandates under common law conditions. The right to publicity of trials rather derives from the public significance of enforcing the legal code. Since the legal process is a universal concern, legal subjects must be empowered not only to bring their own case to court but to have its proceedings open to public scrutiny and to have access to the legal proceedings of other cases.[10] Otherwise, the enforcement of law turns into a private affair, veiled from other legal subjects, whose common entitlement to have their freedoms legally protected gives them an equal stake in seeing the law upheld. To break the veil of privacy, individuals must be enabled either to attend court in person or to be given access to records of court proceedings.

Of course, the publicity of court proceedings is only adequately achieved if what transpires in court is made *intelligibly* available to legal subjects. This requirement is of prime importance to the parties to a case, who only have their due day in court if they are enabled to understand the proceedings. Otherwise, though they may be present, their lack of comprehension leaves them passive recipients of a legal process in which they play no role as knowing and willing participants. To claim that they can then exercise any rights in court is a travesty.[11] By the same token, the public has no genuine access to the court if proceedings are not made accessible in a comprehensible fashion. When comprehensibility can only be achieved with the help of translators or experts, the requirement of publicity makes it a responsibility of the court to make them available to trial parties and audience alike.

Admittedly, during court proceedings conversations may occur and disclosures may be made that are of purely private significance, including exchanges between judges in chambers, jurors in jury rooms, and client and lawyer. Although these communications do not warrant publicity owing to their private character,[12] any aspect of court proceedings that is of legal significance should be made public. This re-

quirement does not mean that all details of wrongs, particularly relating to the identity of endangered informers, victims or minors, must
be made public. In such situations, where the glare of publicity can
cause undue peril and distress, the court has an obligation to show
discretion, provided that, in so doing, it does not cloak in secrecy the
essential facts of the case.[13] In any event, the extent of publicity is not
determined by the preference of individual parties but by the demands
of balancing the right to a proper judicial examination of the facts of a
case with the other rights of individuals.

The Dual Task of the Court

As a public body operating under conditions of publicity, the court has
two tasks to tackle in succession. First, it must conduct an investigation of the facts of the case to determine authoritatively the circumstances of the affair that is to be subsumed under the law. Second, the
court must apply the law to the established facts of the case and come
to a legally binding verdict mandating how the case is to be settled,
including what compensation and punishment are warranted. Taken
together, these two undertakings comprise the trial, the court proceedings that begin with the consideration of the case and conclude
with an authoritative judgment of how the law applies to it.

The different characters of the two constitutive parts of the trial
bear upon the procedures to be followed in each and upon the qualifications of those who are to participate in their execution.

Determining the Facts of the Case and the Role
of the Confession

The first part of the trial, which aims at authoritatively establishing
the facts of the case, has two elements of its own: the proof in court of
what happened and the formal procedures of due process, which insure
that the proof proceeds in conformity with the legal rights of the
parties involved. Insofar as the procedures for proving the facts of the
case are steps that all legal subjects are entitled to pursue in court, they
must be just as legally determined as any other externally enforceable
rights in civil society.[14]

The proof in court itself involves the weighing of evidence for the
sake of establishing the true character of the situation to which the law

is to be applied. Since the law consists in a general rule referring to a type of action in a type of situation, the investigation of the facts of the case cannot restrict itself to disclosing the state of affairs simply in its singularity. The investigation must establish not only the details of what happened but what kind of action transpired, what rights hung in the balance, and what kind of wrong resulted. Moreover, the investigation must move beyond certifying the immediate circumstances of the deed to ascertain the intentions of its author/s and the aspects of the deed and its ramifications that were prefigured in those intentions.[15] This assessment is crucial, since in any case the court must determine whether the wrong at stake was committed nonmaliciously or maliciously. Accordingly, the hearing of evidence must address the kind of purpose and motive behind the deed. Only then can the case be certified to fall under "civil" or "criminal" law with compensation and/or punishment looming as a possible outcome of the application of law.

Since the proof of what happened, both regarding its unique detail and its type, concerns a matter of fact, no other evidence is attainable than testimony of witnesses and the introduction of relevant material exhibits. This limitation holds whether certainty about the facts is obtained immediately, through the sensible intuition of direct witnesses or observation in court of material exhibits, or later, by the mediation of reasoning about the testimony and exhibits.[16] As with all empirical knowledge, the veracity of reported observation is relative to the accuracy and honesty of the witness. The only means for checking such evidence is further testimony or examination of further material exhibits, whose significance is once again relative to the accuracy and honesty of the observation by which it is introduced as evidence. Consequently, the final element in verifying the facts of the case remains subjective conviction and conscience.[17]

The testimony of the participants in the putative wrong may appear to have a privileged position, particularly regarding proof of whether the deed was committed with malice. Confessions especially seem authoritative. Not only can the accused be presumed to have privileged access to his or her own intentions, but if the confession is allowed to decide the facts, the legal process enjoys a threefold satisfaction: first, the convictions of the court and the accused correspond, second, the accused thereby acknowledges that the court has respected his or her right, and third, this harmony is publicly established in the court proceedings, which confirm the right of the accused to be subject only to a verdict that is not foreign to his or her conviction, echoing the provisos of moral accountability.[18]

However, if confession is granted the exclusive privilege of providing sufficient evidence to determine whether a wrong has been committed with or without malice, then the judicial process risks being stymied by the refusal of the accused to plead guilty, a prospect all the more likely when, in a criminal case, a guilty defendant has already shown willingness to act against right and can hardly be expected to relish imposing punishment upon him or herself.[19] The only way to overcome such refusal would be to employ torture, but torture can neither be trusted to discriminate between the innocent and the guilty nor be counted upon to secure confessions before killing the accused.[20]

Even if confession is not given exclusive privilege to establish the intentions of the accused, it must still be recognized that any confession may be just as inaccurate or dishonest as the report of any other witness. Not only may defendants be sincerely deluded or mistaken about what they have done or seen, but they may be sheltering others from blame or sheltering themselves in plea bargaining from the risk of greater punishment. Consequently, the proof of the facts of the case should not automatically hang upon the confessions of accused parties. Such privileging of avowals of guilt is unjustly allowed to occur when confession is made a condition for a guilty verdict or when defendants can plead guilty and put an end to any public, too, is cheatedcourt of the facts of the case.[21] Either way, arbitrary constraints are put upon individuals' right to have the facts of the case fully investigated.[22] Since any trial in civil society has a public significance reflected in the publicity under which it proceeds, the public, too, is cheated.[23] Consequently, the practice of having criminal defendants enter a plea of guilty or not guilty in order to decide the path of court proceedings should be abandoned. It is worth noting that this has already been done in Continental legal systems: in Germany, for instance, the guilty plea is absent and all cases are duly tried whether or not confessions are forthcoming.[24]

Similar considerations weigh against any right of an accused against self-incrimination. Arguments in behalf of such an alleged right have ordinarily followed Hobbes's lead and appealed to the logic of social contract, according to which no individuals can be obliged by the legal process to put their life and liberty in jeopardy when the only rationale for subjecting themselves to the authority of a civil government was self-preservation.[25] Given, however, that social contract theory is undermined by foundational dilemmas[26] and that the authority of law in civil society does not rest upon the consent of individuals, such rationales have no more validity than Beccaria's argument against capital punishment, which analogously appeals to social contract.

Objections fare no better when they appeal to the integrity of personhood and moral subjectivity, not as allegedly given by nature but as determined in the interactions constitutive of property relations and moral accountability.[27] The fact that impositions upon choice are not illegitimate in principle becomes evident once one recognizes that right and duty go together and that persons can therefore only exercise their entitled freedoms within a framework obliging them to restrict their conduct in function of upholding the rights of others.

Compelling individuals either to perjure themselves or to contribute to their own conviction hardly places them in the predicament of choosing between undermining their own moral dignity or sacrificing their entire self to public authority.[28] Far from involving a lamentable clash of rights, the elimination of the "right" against self-incrimination gives defendants the opportunity to affirm their integrity and legal autonomy at once. By accepting responsibility for their wrongs, cooperating with the proof of the facts, and submitting to adjudication and possible punishment, defendants affirm their correlative right and duty as accountable legal subjects and are publicly recognized in this free capacity. In so doing, they testify to how neither self-interest nor self-preservation are the unconditional end of justice, let alone the pillar of human dignity.

However, it would be wrong to argue conversely against the right of the accused to refuse to testify in court on the ground that this right permits the facts of the case to be determined independently of confession.[29] Since confession has no exclusive privilege as evidence of the purpose and intention of the accused, the right against self-incrimination must be challenged on other grounds.

The basic ground is straightforward enough: judicial justice demands that the truth of the case be brought to light, and absolving the accused from the duty to testify does not serve that requirement. Admittedly, since the interest of the accused may well be to portray him or herself as innocent, self-incrimination is not to be expected,[30] except when the accused has chosen the path of right or seeks to protect the actual guilty party or pleads guilty to a lesser charge to escape a greater punishment. The demand that the accused testify may thus seem a severe demand, but can it be more something of subjective interest than a matter of justice, as Hegel suggests?[31]

If defendants are not granted a right against self-incrimination, they might appear to be prey to torture. This risk can be kept at bay, however, simply by outlawing and strictly punishing torture[32] and by not giving confession any automatic privilege in deciding the outcome of cases. Instead of facing torture, defendants would have three options when called upon to testify: to tell the truth as they see it, to lie, or to stand in contempt of court for refusal to testify. No injustice occurs by their avowing the truth, of their innocence or of their guilt. If they are found to have lied in court, however, they deserve to be punished for the wrong of acting with malice against the laws of due process, which oblige witnesses not to commit perjury. It might be objected that this subjects defendants to a double punishment. But the double punishment only occurs if the accused are found to be guilty and found to have committed perjury, a conjunction that is hardly automatic. Nor does the obligation to testify if subpoenaed in any way undermine the ability of a defendant to have evidence thoroughly and fairly marshaled before the court. On the contrary, allowing defendants to refuse to testify without being held in contempt of court is itself an obstacle to a full and thorough hearing of all the relevant evidence. However, since the defendant's testimony has no special privilege, it provides only one more piece of the puzzle, requiring as much testing as any other evidence.[33] Hence, the principle of treating an accused as innocent until proven guilty remains in force, even when the defendant confesses in court.

An analogous issue concerns the rights of confidentiality of lawyers and their clients. If such rights are forfeited by allowing lawyers to be subpoenaed to testify on what clients have admitted to them, then clients would seem to be in a position where their right to counsel conflicts with any right against self-incrimination.[34] Yet if the right against self-incrimination is itself bogus, then clients are simply faced with the choice of telling their counsel the truth and facing the legal consequences or deceiving counsel and court alike. Admittedly, eliminating rights against self-incrimination and lawyer-client confidences may lead accused individuals to withhold information they mistakenly think is incriminating, to the detriment of their defense.[35] However, these measures may just as well promote fuller disclosures that promote the rights of all.

By the same token, plaintiffs should not be allowed the final say in specifying the character of the alleged wrong. Giving them the power to define once and for all the charges equally deprives the public and other parties to the trial of a due investigation of the facts of the case. Not only may the plaintiff honestly or dishonestly misconstrue what occurred but scrutiny of evidence in court may reveal new perspectives that warrant revising the charges. Hence, if the examination of evidence in court indicates that the alleged wrong is of a different sort, legal justice would be obstructed if the court were unable to alter the charge and proceed to a proper proof of its truth.[36] Such revisions of the charges are the responsibility of the judge presiding over the hearing of evidence, who has a duty to guide the court proceedings in accord with the demand to have the facts of the case duly investigated. Continental legal systems, such as that of Germany, have shown proper sense in granting judges this power to alter charges.[37]

Given the fallibility of plaintiff and accused, as well as of every other witness, it is futile to hope to eliminate all uncertainty regarding factual knowledge of the case. The proof of what happened can at best depend upon a judgment beyond reasonable, but not beyond all possible, doubt. Since justice requires that wrong be righted through legal enforcement, any hesitation due to the inability to overcome *all* doubt about the facts of a case robs individuals of their right to a trial. Although new revelations can always arise that call into question past judicial examinations, whatever the court duly establishes to be the facts counts as objectively valid until further court proceedings certify the new information.

Since coming to a judgment concerning the facts of the case is a matter of arriving at factual knowledge based upon empirical observation, any mature, sane rational agent is competent to perform that task. Although this judgment is informed by the basic legal categories that permit identifying the kind of right at issue (i.e., title of ownership, contract, marriage agreement, adoption, etc.) and the type of wrong (nonmalicious, fraud, or crime), the determination of the facts of the case itself involves no pronouncement of law.[38] Consequently, those who sit in judgment upon the hearing of evidence and come to an authoritative verdict concerning what occurred need not have any special legal training.

The Right of Due Process and the Conditions of Its Realization

Legal expertise is not, however, irrelevant to the investigation in court of the facts of the case. That court examination must itself follow a legally defined procedure respecting the right of all parties. Otherwise, the right to a just trial has no objective or universally binding content. Accordingly, laws of trial procedure governing the admission of evidence and the examination of witnesses are necessary to insure that the facts of the case are thoroughly investigated and that the court restricts its scrutiny to those facts that pertain to the enforcement of law.

Furthermore, if the parties to the case are to exercise their right to participate in court, they must be adequately informed of the rules of trial procedure and furnished with whatever resources are necessary to enable them to present evidence in court. The latter entails defraying, when necessary, the costs of securing witnesses, whether they are expert or lay individuals, and of obtaining, introducing, and examining material exhibits. Moreover, to the degree that any of these functions requires the aid of legal experts, such expertise must be made affordably available to all parties without prejudice to quality and quantity. Since this condition follows from the exigence of realizing the right of individuals to a proper examination of the facts of their case, it is an exigence generic to any trial, no matter what kind of law and what kind of wrong is at stake. Any legal system that guarantees legal aid only in criminal cases violates this basic requirement of legal justice.

The body of laws that mandates these measures for guaranteeing the trial rights of individuals comprises standards of due process, to whose application every legal subject is entitled. Without being able to exercise these rights to due process, individuals are deprived of their basic legal right to prove their rights in court and have them legally enforced.[39]

Consequently, some public figure or figures must preside over the hearing of evidence to insure that trial procedures are properly followed. To fill this role of presiding judge requires knowledge of the laws of due process and the court procedures by which they are enforced. Accordingly, whoever is charged with this presiding role must either be publicly certified to possess the requisite legal expertise or be provided with publicly certified expert advisors. Either way, the presiding judge serves as an impartial organ of legality, guiding the legal proceedings to duly prepare the case for subsumption under the law, bringing to culmination the proof that renders the alleged infringement of right a recognized fact with recognized universal qualities to which law can apply.[40]

The constitutive structure of the first stage of the trial thus allows for several possible organizations of the court.[41] Because those charged with judging the facts of the case may or may not be legal experts, whereas the court officials presiding over the hearing of evidence must either be judicial experts or have expert advice, the trial may employ a jury of lay individuals presided over by legal experts, a jury of lay individuals who either preside themselves over the hearing with the aid of legal experts or are presided over by other lay individuals having judicial advisers, or the same or different legal experts to decide the facts and preside over the hearing of evidence.

Procedural Abuse and the Rationale for Equity

No matter how configured, the court cannot escape the possibility of parties to the trial using their rights of due process to obstruct the judicial righting of wrong. This possibility cannot be precluded simply because the legal process is itself something external to the rights it seeks to uphold. Although engaging in legal procedures is itself a right, it remains a means to promote an end distinct from itself. Consequently, there can be no guarantee that employment of this means will automatically promote the end for which it is designed.[42] Instead of serving right, litigation may become a tool of undeserved harassment, just as trial prerogatives and "legal technicalities" may be used to evade punishment or responsibility for compensation. In these respects, the legal process cannot help but be an "imperfect procedure,"[43] whose outcome may well betray the innocent and favor the guilty and negligent even though the court verdict commands binding authority. This predicament engenders an apparent conflict of rights, where the right to due process interferes with the right to have one's property, family, and economic entitlements legally enforced.

How can this conflict be resolved? A common remedy, for which Hegel argues, is recourse to equity, where the court offers the parties to a trial the option of settling the case in the interest of right without strict adherence to the formalities of due process. Through this device of an equity settlement, the substance of the case is allowed to prevail over the external obstructions of court procedure.[44] As Hegel points out, the appeal to equity can operate in two complementary ways. Equity can operate in respect to content, so as to allow for a departure from the imperatives of strict right in the interests of other normative considerations. Alternately, equity can function in respect to form, so as to allow the formalities of court procedure to be bypassed.[45]

Since any such deviations from legally specified grounds of right and court procedures are motivated by the unique predicament of the case, they cannot count as universal legal pronouncements that either rescind or revise prior law.[46] If, instead, equity decisions are treated as binding precedents, they forfeit their very own status as deviations from law by becoming fixtures of a new common law, suffering from the same problems of indeterminacy that haunt any uncodified legal rules.

By the same token, if the recourse to equity fosters an independent system of equity courts, as occurred, for example, in Britain and in the United States,[47] it undermines its own mission by becoming merely an additional court with its own rules of procedure subject to the same misuse as those of its nonequity counterpart. It is thus no surprise that Kant, for one, could consider a court of equity inherently contradictory.[48]

Indeed, a reversion to ordinary court difficulties is prevented only if an equity remedy consists either in an informal out-of-court settlement or in a judicial decision acknowledging exceptional reasons for deviating from legal grounds and procedures. In such cases, four circumstances save the equity decision from simply being a usurpation of legal right: one, the equity process proceeds only with the consent of the parties to the case, who have had the opportunity to make an informed free choice between sticking with strict due process or an equity settlement,[49] two, it is delivered with the authorization of the court, three, it appeals to the content of the enforceable rights of civil society, rights that should already be enshrined in the legal code, and, four, it accordingly does not degenerate into an arbitration of conflicting interests, whose outcome reflects only the relative bargaining strength of the disputants, rather than their submission to the law.[50]

The first proviso, that the equity process can only proceed with the consent of the parties to the case, might appear to limit drastically appeals to equity, since one party often has an advantage to gain from employing due process to prevent the other party from attaining the legal remedy it deserves. Yet even if both parties directly benefit from equity only in exceptional cases, civil society has an interest in preventing legal formalities from obstructing right, both because of the social costs incurred and because of the imperative to have legality be an instrument for enforcing right.

Consequently, a way is needed to resolve the problems that equity addresses without being hamstrung by the arbitrariness of consent to particular equity settlements. The institution of "no-fault" publicly guaranteed compensation of particular wrongs provides an appropriate solution. By being integrated within the legal code, this approach can overcome the possible misuse of due process to evade responsibility for compensation without introducing methods that deviate from legal practice or remain hostage to subjective preference. By effectively supplanting tort litigation with a system of social insurance, this system allows public authority to meet its obligation to guarantee that the victims of malicious or nonmalicious wrongs receive due compensation even when it cannot be obtained from the perpetrators, either because of the latter's lack of sufficient resources or because of the difficulties of obtaining remedy through tort litigation. Since the right of members of civil society includes legal protection of their person and property, their family welfare, and their economic well-being, public authority can extend the guarantees of "no-fault" compensation under the aegis of a comprehensive accident insurance that covers all injuries, disabilities, and property damages, whether they are caused by nature or other agents. Such an undertaking, heralded by recent legislation in New Zealand,[51] further narrows the opportunities for right to suffer at the hands of strict adherence to due process. Although such no-fault social insurance overrides the strict liability of nonmalicious wrong, transferring responsibility for compensation from the individual nonmalicious "wrongdoer" to the public, it does so for the sake of upholding the rights of all in civil society. Like every legitimate restriction upon property right, this measure limits particular dimensions of right for the sake of right's own general realization.

Application of the Law

Once the examination of evidence has led to a determination of the facts of the case, the trial enters its second stage, during which the court must subsume these established facts under the law and reach a decision redressing the wrong and reestablishing right.[52] The resulting verdict therefore contains two sides, bringing to culmination the dual tasks of the trial: it gives expression to the universal character of the case at hand and then mandates how the law, in addressing that universal character, dictates how right is to be reestablished in this individual instance.[53]

Although the preceding investigation of the facts is guided by general notions of what rights are putatively at stake and what types of wrong may have transpired, it confines itself to certifying what happened and demands nothing but ordinary understanding. By contrast, to judge how the case falls under the law requires special knowledge of the legal code. Although the legal code should be accessible to all legal subjects, the complexity of civil society entails that knowledge of the legal code will likely depend upon legal expertise. Consequently, whoever is charged with applying the law to the established facts of the case must either have legal expertise or be provided with legal advice.

Whatever their qualifications, those who judge the case come to a decision containing two elements: the law to be applied and the subjective discretion bridging the gap between the universality of legal rule and the contingent individuality of the established facts of the case. Because the law only refers to general types of conduct and entitlements, its application to contingent individual cases can never rely upon deduction to the exclusion of subjective discretion of judicial judgment.[54] The latter component cannot be eliminated, for any supervening control will have to employ the same subjective discretion in applying the law to the individual judicial conduct of the judge.[55] At every level of judicial application, judges must do what neither the law nor any law-governed calculation can ever accomplish by itself, namely, declare how a legal norm relates to a contingent situation.[56] The judgment of the court contributes this service, and the crux of judicial argument revolves around giving reasons for how antecedently determinate laws apply to an individual case rather than giving reasons that determine law itself.

Accordingly, judicial argument cannot properly refer to prior judicial decisions as a source for determining the meaning of the law. Moreover, since each case is unique, no prior judicial decision can provide a rule for deducing how a current case should be decided. At best, reference to prior decisions can only serve as analogical illustrations[57] of the kind of judgment that now must once more independently apply the law within the prevailing understanding of how the legal code posits right.

Undeniably, the element of law enters in only as it is interpreted by the judge. Yet, as the arguments against rule skepticism suggest, judicial interpretation cannot help but be circumscribed by limits imposed by the shared recognition ingredient in the ethical community of legality. Judges can only exercise their authoritative role upon the basis of an antecedently recognized interpretation of the laws specifying the legal process as well as of the body of the legal code that comprises the law that judges are authorized to apply. If they ignore this systemic unity, their judgment loses its public stature and the binding privilege it enjoys. Moreover, the legal code itself only counts to the degree that it commands enough univocal recognition to escape desuetude. Judges are bound to refer to this recognized significance rather than to any contingent factors underlying the genesis of the legal code.[58]

In these respects, Hegel can rightly maintain that public opinion, served by the publicity of judicial decisions,[59] acts as a counterweight to the opinion of the court.[60] For if publicized court decisions deviate too far from what is publicly acknowledged as the law, judges risk losing the recognition on which their authority rests. Hence, although the principles of right remain the ultimate standard for determining the validity of law, the most just laws exercise no actual authority unless legal subjects preponderantly recognize their common significance and their due application by the court and show this recognition in a preponderant degree of rectitude.

These considerations themselves provide no reason why the same individuals cannot preside over the hearing of evidence and apply the law, and no reason why those serving as judges cannot do so with legal expertise of their own or as lay individuals assisted by expert advisors. In each case, judicial decision operates with the same elements and within the same confines. Moreover, the distinct functions of the trial in no way preclude judges from arriving at decisions with or without a separate lay jury to determine the facts of the case.

Should Juries Be Mandatory in All Trials?

Do other aspects of legal rights in civil society prescribe a more narrow organization of the court, making jury trials not just one possibility among others, but a mandatory feature of due process? De Tocqueville and others [61] have argued that jury trials are to be preferred because they serve as organs of democracy, both extending democratic empowerment and providing training grounds for popular participation. Similar considerations underlie arguments for the popular election of judges and for the elimination of legal qualifications that exclude lay judges.

These measures might appear to concern self-government insofar as they involve the enforcement of law and thereby seem to fall within the executive branch of government. Yet law in civil society is not determined in terms of political relations; it only posits the prepolitical rights of property owners, family members, economic agents, and legal subjects, which have a global dimension applying to citizens and non-citizens alike. Consequently, the exercise of legal functions is far from identical with the reflexive operations of self-rule, whose every activity involves citizens imposing order upon themselves and the body politic in which their political engagement proceeds. Moreover, if court functions were to be treated as political processes, the imperatives of collective self-rule would exercise direct hegemony, undercutting any distinct sphere of play for the different modes of freedom constitutive of civil institutions. And from a systematic point of view, even if the above rationales for jury trials possess merit, [62] they all depend upon the determination of valid political institutions, which itself presupposes how law is determined in civil society. Hence, what must first be established is whether, within the context of civil society, jury trials have any exclusive authority.

Do, then, the legal imperatives of civil association accord preeminence to jury trials? A commonly cited ground for privileging jury trials is the alleged principle that judges should be peers of the accused. This notion is, as Hegel points out, doubly confused. First, it leaves undefined exactly what a peer is supposed to be. In civil society, no judge can fail to be a peer of the accused insofar as all members count as free and equal persons, moral subjects, potential family members, and economic agents. Yet if being a peer involves something more particular than exercising the rights common to all members of civil society, what, if any, particular differences deserve to be privileged when it comes to deciding the facts of a case in court? If criminals do not deserve to be exclusively judged by criminals,[63] how should jury membership be defined? Is class the appropriate measure, or gender, sexual orientation, race, religion, ethnic identity, age, or something else? Although one might be tempted to argue that only peers of an accused can judge without prejudice, one could maintain equally that peers, however defined, may just as well be partial to the accused.[64] Moreover, if the notion of being judged by one's "peers" is imprecise and without any automatic connection to the impartial justice of rule by law, the institution of a jury does not even concern the identity of judges, since what the jury will decide are the facts of the case, not how the law applies to them.[65]

Does a less problematic justification for jury trials lie in concern for a separation of judicial powers, where juries are warranted to the degree that they afford civilians protection from the arbitrariness of public officials? Yet do legal subjects need such protection in the first place? If the officials who bring cases to court are distinct from those who try them, is not the root of a conflict of interest largely overcome? Moreover, why should a body of jurors be any more impartial than a judge, whose selection and longevity in office could be determined in any number of ways to neutralize the arrogance of power?

Hegel, for one, attempts to sidestep these difficulties and still adamantly argue that the rights of legal subjects in civil society mandate trial by jury. He recognizes that trial by jury is a viable option because the investigation of the facts of the case can be performed by any educated person.[66] Yet since this circumstance only allows for jury trials but does not make them mandatory for accomplishing the first stage of judicial proceedings, Hegel reaches further. He claims that the ultimate rationale for jury trials lies in the right of each individual agent to be able to know and believe in the verdict that has been decreed in his or her case.[67] This right is attributed to subjective consciousness, suggesting that it is a legal embodiment of the right of moral agency to be held accountable only for those aspects of a deed and its ramifications that are prefigured in the purpose and motive of the moral subject and are accompanied by knowledge of the right or wrong of the correspondingly circumscribed action. Although this right of subjective agency may apply to moral conduct, it is far from self-evident how it is reaffirmed by jury trials, either at all or exclusively.

If this right were to be taken literally as a governing principle of court procedure, trial verdicts would be legitimate only when they conformed to whatever the accused avowed. Otherwise, the only conviction that would count would be that of the judge, withdrawing recognition of the accused's accountability as a moral subject.[68] As Hegel himself points out, such a connection mistakenly privileges the authority of confession, ignoring how guilty pleas may be made in bad faith or through self-delusion, while encouraging recourse to torture as an inescapable instrument of justice, despite its inability to guarantee the guilt of whoever confesses, let alone survival of its own rigors.

Consequently, if the right of subjective consciousness is to apply to court verdicts, it must be detached from the immediate conviction of the accused yet still be identifiable with the latter's conscience. Hegel maintains that the jury provides exactly what is needed: a suitably surrogate conscience, whose lay members' determination of the facts of the case provides an authoritative avowal of responsibility, giving expression to the point of view of the accused but purifying it of the elements of subjective delusion and dishonesty. Moreover, if the jury is composed of members from the same estate as the accused, it will not only share in the defendant's outlook but command the trust of the accused, who will thereby recognize his or her own conviction in the jurors' verdict.[69]

It is tempting to dismiss Hegel's argument on the grounds that, even if it held, it would hardly give a blanket authorization for jury trials. Because the whole thrust of Hegel's rationale revolves around honoring the right of the accused to have the verdict of the court accord with his or her conscience,[70] it would seem to apply only to criminal cases, where the intent of the accused plays a determining role in deciding guilt or innocence and any corresponding punishment. Since no malice is involved in civil cases, their settlement in court is not defined in any positive way by the intentions of the interested parties.

Nevertheless, purpose and intention do play a role in trials of nonmalicious wrongs, since only with an examination of the aims and motives of the litigants can the court establish whether negligence or malice are to be excluded as contributing factors to the infringement of right. Hence, if Hegel's argument rings true, jury trials should be mandatory for civil cases as well.

Yet does the right of subjective conviction to which Hegel appeals have a constitutive role to play in court proceedings, and, if so, does it require a jury trial? Hegel presumes that without juries, courts must demand confessions from defendants, opening the door to torture,[71] since otherwise verdicts will be handed down that need not conform to the publicly avowed conviction of the accused. The freedom of the accused can only be respected by ensuring that the established wrong for which the defendant is held responsible accords with what the defendant intended, and without juries stepping in as a surrogate voice for the aims and motives of the defendant, only a confession can certify that the accountability of the accused is properly recognized.

Admittedly, how the accused viewed their own deed is a crucial element in the facts of a case, given how the purpose and intention of the agent are decisive for identifying an act as malicious or non-malicious wrong. However, owing to the very limits of the authority of confession that Hegel himself has underlined, what the defendant publicly avows does not necessarily define the limits of the accused's accountability.

Moreover, why is a jury privileged to speak for the defendant when a judge is not? As Hegel himself has shown, being a peer of the defendant is not only a hopelessly vague qualification but no guarantee of impartiality or trust. Anyway, a judge can just as easily be a peer of the accused as a group of jurors, if peerage is defined in terms of particular differences of race, gender, religion, or social origin. This possibility is particularly likely when judges can be legal experts or lay individuals with expert advice. It is worth noting that Hegel privileges estate membership as the particular factor on which trust between juror and accused can be based,[72] appealing to a feudal category that combines birthright with social and political privilege in a way that contradicts the freedoms of civil society and the state, as well as the demarcation of those two institutional domains.[73] Even if Hegel's estate division were translated into the more appropriate idiom of class divisions, there would still be neither any necessity that its commonality of economic need and interest secures a common outlook and trust between juror and accused, nor any guarantee that judges could not share the same class background as the accused.

Furthermore, if the jury qualifies as the surrogate voice of the defendant because it has judiciously weighed the evidence concerning purpose and motive, what prevents one or more judges from doing the same? As long as judges are not charged with bringing indictments, why should they be any more likely to have a conflict of interest than a juror? Moreover, since judges can be selected in ways that either shield them from pressure from private interests or make them responsible to public opinion, why must they constitute a force any more alien to the defendant than the jurors?

Hegel does add one further justification for jury trials that might escape these objections. Although his appeal to the right of subjective freedom involves a denial that jury trials can be defended as a means for permitting justice to be administered in a more impartial manner,[74] he elsewhere maintains that unless those who determine the facts do not also impose the penalty, they cannot be impartial.[75] But why should disposing over the authority to perform both functions of the trial undermine impartiality? If one body of individuals can impartially establish the facts of the case, including the aims and motives of the accused, why cannot that same group apply the law fairly, assuming that they either are legal experts or are afforded expert advice?

Hegel maintains that if the judge takes over the function of the jury, the judge is liable to determine the facts of the case in view of their legal consequences.[76] Yet, as Hegel admits, jurors may do so just as well, especially when the punishments are severe.[77] Moreover, there is no reason for a judge's view of the legal consequences of a case to prejudice how that judge determines the facts unless the judge is already biased for or against the defendant, which need not be any more likely than the bias of a jury.

The crucial point is that the functions of determining the facts of the case and subsuming it under the law are completely different in character. Hegel argues that they are not only different, but opposed, because, in impartially applying the law, the judge must end up taking sides against one of the parties, whereas in determining the facts of the case, the standpoint of the defendant is expressed.[78] However, this supposed opposition is actually overcome: the application of the law only confirms the legal ramifications of the finding of the facts (including the determination of what the accused intended), whether the accused is found guilty or innocent of a crime and/or responsible or not responsible for compensation.

Consequently, the two functions of the trial do not "prejudice" the execution of one another in any necessary fashion, whether or not they are performed by different individuals. If the establishment of the facts of the case dictated exactly how the law were to be applied, judicial discretion would be eliminated. Since, however, recourse to subjective judgment cannot be escaped, there is no determinate way in which judges' decision is swayed by whether they have or have not also decided the facts of the case.

As a result, as long as the legal system guarantees that litigants know the law, understand the court proceedings, and dispose of resources to take full advantage of due process, and as long as the system guarantees that the court fully investigates the facts of the case and duly applies the law, the right of subjective accountability can be upheld with or without a jury trial.[79]

Judge or jury, should those who come to a verdict be required to decide the case by unanimous decision? The demand for unanimity, commonly made in jury trials in Britain and the United States, reflects the requirement that the verdict have an objective certainty signaled in the agreement of each and every juror's subjective certainty.[80] Yet why should unanimity be any more a guarantee of objectivity than the requirement of a majority decision, as practiced in France? By itself, unanimity, like majority decision, is insufficient unless the matter of agreement conforms to the circumstances themselves.[81] Since, however, justice entails that a requirement be employed in a uniform way for all legal subjects, it is a matter of convention whether unanimous or majority decision is binding. No matter what decision principle is accepted, the verdict remains a judgment resting on the subjective conviction of those who uphold it, with the qualification that their conviction is entitled to pronounce what counts for the court.[82]

Grounds for Appeal and Retrial

Since adherence to proper court procedures is itself a matter of right that therefore must be specified by law, provision must be made for authoritatively judging and enforcing the court's own rectitude. Such an authoritative review must itself take the form of a trial subject to all the prescriptions applying to court procedures in general. The review must be public, parties to it must be afforded sufficient resources to enable their due participation, and it must follow legally specified procedures spelling out how prior court decisions are to be brought to appeal, how such verdicts are to be reexamined and judged, and how any retrials are to be conducted. Given the constitutive tasks of the legal process, every trial is subject to review on three grounds: that new evidence has surfaced that warrants a reinvestigation of the facts of the case, that due process was not properly followed in the prior investigation of the facts, and that the judge flagrantly misapplied the law. The court investigation of each of these bases of appeal does not involve questions of law merely. Like any other trial, an appeal has two successive tasks: first, to ascertain the facts of the case, which here concern what happened at the prior trial and any new evidence, and second, to apply the law to those authoritatively established facts. The same qualifications, then, apply to the definition of who is fit to perform these two functions. In principle, courts of appeal can employ the same or different groups of legal experts to decide the facts and apply the law, employ the same or different lay individuals to decide the facts and apply the law with expert advisors, or employ lay jurors to decide the facts and legal experts to apply the law.

Since each verdict of appeal can itself be questioned on the same three grounds of new evidence, violation of due process, and flagrant misapplication of law, the only way an endless series of reviews can be avoided is if a final court of appeal is granted ultimate say. Because trial verdicts have binding authority unless they are overturned by further court decisions, the same case cannot be retried after appeals have been exhausted. Accordingly, all legal subjects have a right to protection from double jeopardy.

The Differentiation of Civil and Criminal Court Procedure

All the foregoing features of the legal process apply equally to the different branches of law since, whether property, family, or economic rights are at stake, trying a case involves the same issues of publicity, factual discovery, due process, and application of the law. Should court procedures nonetheless be differentiated according to the type of wrong that is to be remedied?

Typically, modern trial procedures have been distinguished according to whether a civil or criminal case is before the court. This distinction rests upon the difference between nonmalicious and malicious wrongs.[83] Civil cases involve situations in which plaintiffs either seek some remedy for infringements of right unintentionally caused by the person or property of defendants or claim entitlements that are disputed by another party. In either case, the agent from whom restitution or compensation is sought is accused of nonmaliciously violating the rights of the plaintiff. By contrast, criminal cases involve circumstances where the accused has intentionally violated another's rights, either through fraud or open coercion.

In both civil and criminal cases, accusations must be brought to court, the facts must be proven, and the law must be applied to the established state of affairs. Does, however, the presence or absence of malice require a different approach for any of these steps in the legal process? Or should the example of ancient Greek law be followed, where civil and criminal law are not distinguished, and, to paraphrase Aristotle's formulation, corrective justice applies in the same way, whether the case involves voluntary or involuntary transactions (i.e., contract or fraud, theft and assault), as if crimes and civil offenses or punishment and compensation could be conflated?[84]

Modern practice does generally distinguish civil and criminal procedures in several salient ways.[85] Ordinarily crimes are prosecuted by public prosecutors, whereas individuals bring civil offenses to trial. In criminal cases, prosecutions can only be withdrawn by the public prosecutor, whereas civil actions can only be withdrawn by private plaintiffs, not by any public authority. Furthermore, criminal and civil prosecutions are pursued in different courts, with criminal courts more often employing juries and requiring stricter rules of evidence than is the case in civil courts. Moreover, in the United States at least, defendants in criminal cases are guaranteed legal representation at public expense, whereas litigants in civil cases enjoy no such guarantee. When civil and criminal courts apply the law, only recompense can be mandated in civil cases, whereas punishment can be meted out in criminal cases. Finally, convicted criminals can be pardoned by legal authorities but not by private individuals, whereas civil offenses can be absolved by private plaintiffs but not by public officials.

Do these common distinctions between civil and criminal procedure accord with right or should they be revised and amended? Since criminal acts violate not only the legal rights of particular individuals but law itself, criminal prosecution should be a public responsibility, independent of the initiative or consent of the victim. Although prosecutions may be handicapped by a victim's unwillingness to provide evidence, prosecution should not be predicated upon whether a victim decides to press charges. Nor should the character of the charges be contingent upon how the victim chooses to formulate them. If the injury to law is to be duly remedied in accord with its public character, criminal prosecutions must be freed of these shackles to the private discretion of victims. Otherwise the righting of criminal wrong retains a vestige of revenge, and due process remains hostage to the subjective preference of victims.[86] To overcome this deformation of criminal procedure, which still plagues American legal practice, public authorities must take charge of preparing indictments and pursuing prosecution in court,[87] whereas presiding judges must ensure that the charges are properly construed, given the course of the trial examination of the facts of the case. By the same token, if a prosecution is to be withdrawn, it should only be withdrawn by the public prosecutor because of insufficient admissible evidence and not in deference to the preferences of victims or any other private party. Similarly, to dismiss charges in court should be the prerogative only of the presiding judge, who is obliged to throw a criminal case out of court when it clearly cannot be duly proven in court. Further, the pardon of convicted criminals cannot depend upon the whim of victims or any other private individuals without undermining the public character of punishment. If pardon is at all admissible, it can only be based upon the decision of duly empowered legal authorities. Of course, the general right of individuals to due process entitles any defendant to legal counsel and whatever preparatory investigation is necessary to ensure that the facts of the case are fairly investigated.

When a civil case revolves around conflicting claims of right, it would appear that very different procedures should be followed. The existence of such a conflict is predicated upon the litigants' resolve to advance opposing interpretations of each others' entitlements. Consequently, the wrong is immediately removed if the litigants come to an agreement whereby one party takes back its contentious claim and recognizes the interpretation of the other party. For this reason, the prosecution of such a civil offense should be left to the initiative of the private parties involved, who may accordingly withdraw charges the moment one retracts its conflicting claim.[88] However, contrary to the practice of the United States, litigants in such civil cases still have a right to legal counsel and any preparatory investigation, regardless of their private means, since due process requires that their personal resources not prejudice their ability to uphold their rights in court. To ignore this entitlement is tantamount to withdrawing recognition of every legal right of individuals in civil society, each of which can be violated just as much nonmaliciously as maliciously.

What, however, of those civil cases that involve not conflicting claims but accidents causing harm to the person and property of individuals, and/or to the well-being of their family and economic affairs? Such civil offenses, which Hegel for one tends to neglect, can largely be removed from tort litigation through a system of social insurance. Such a system not only saves individuals and civil society from incurring significant legal expenses but also greatly facilitates the ability of victims to receive prompt compensation, circumventing the risk of having due process used against them by resourceful plaintiffs. Yet what if these equity considerations do not entirely stop accident claims from being filed in court? Are the prosecutions of these civil offenses to be left the responsibility of the victim? And should victims be permitted to withdraw charges if they please?

Such cases have a certain objectivity lacking in civil disputes where the subjective resolve to interpret one's rights in conflict with another's is the ground of the wrong. The harm incurred through accident cannot be removed by reaching an agreement about the rights of the victim. The fact of the harm mandates that compensation is due and must be provided. The right of accident victims to have their loss remedied in court would be impeded if responsibility for bringing suit rested solely with them and no public guarantee were offered of the means for pursuing the case when the victim was hampered by injury or lack of resources.

Yet if such guarantees are provided is there any reason to place the prosecution of such civil offenses in public hands and to prevent victims from withdrawing claims for compensation if they choose? No one has a right to undermine one's own freedoms. If victims refuse compensation when this refusal prevents them from exercising their rights or fulfilling their duties to others, then the court has a responsibility to provide for them. In such conditions, victims have neither the authority to refuse to sue nor the power to withdraw civil suits.

Public authority must intercede in their behalf as custodians of their autonomy. When the conditions of autonomy are not at stake, however, the refusal to receive compensation is tantamount to giving away alienable property to which one may prove to be entitled. Since that certainly falls within the prerogatives of ownership, accident victims would appear to be entitled to avoid filing suit and to refuse compensation when such decisions neither undermine their autonomy as owner, moral subject, family member, and economic agent, nor undermine the welfare of their dependents.

Granted these provisos for trying civil offenses, are there any grounds for having different standards for the investigation of the facts of a case, including the use of a lay jury? Contemporary practice seems to support the notion that rules of evidence should be stricter in criminal trials, and, following the example of Britain, that jury trials are less expendable in criminal cases. But why should the weighing of evidence be any less stringent in a civil case? The same violation of an individual's right can be inflicted maliciously or nonmaliciously, and identifying that violation as of one or the other type requires the same inquiry into purpose and motive. Consequently, the investigation of the facts is completely parallel in either type of case, which would seem to call for common rules of evidence and a common instrument for reaching a verdict on the facts.

If, however, stricter rules of evidence are called for in jury trials because lay jurors are less trained to ignore hearsay and leading questions,[89] this requirement still does not divide civil from criminal procedure, since civil offenses and crimes can both be tried with or without juries.

The preceding consideration does not uphold de Toqueville's argument for extending jury trials from criminal to civil cases. His argument rests upon the political consideration that such an extension allows juries to preside over the everyday, rather than the exceptional, affairs of all, thereby fostering among the citizenry a more thorough sense of equity, judicial judgment, and democratic participation.[90] What the parallel in the investigation of the facts in civil and criminal cases rather supports is allowing civil and criminal courts to employ the same organization, be it with or without juries.

The Controversy between the *"Inquisitorial"* and *"Adversary"* Systems of Court Procedure

Given the constitutive features of a just legal process and the proper differentiation between civil and criminal trials, do either the inquisitorial or adversary systems of court procedure warrant acceptance, let alone preferential adoption?[91] In the inquisitorial system,[92] judges actively lead the investigation of the facts of the case, supervising the formulation of charges, selecting and interrogating witnesses (including expert authorities), and insuring that lawyers serve as nonpartisan members of the court, devoted to uncovering the facts in conformity with due process. Although lawyers have the option of calling witnesses on their own, they are prohibited from coaching them, defer most questioning to the judge, and are forbidden to conceal relevant information or to receive contingency fees tied to the victory of their client. By contrast, the adversary system restricts the judge to the role of impartial umpire of a combat between opposing lawyers. The latter adversaries exercise exclusive power to call, coach, and interrogate witnesses, including whatever experts they can muster. They serve throughout as partisan advocates of their clients, even when this partisanship entails withholding information, pleading the innocence of the guilty, and receiving contingency fees dependent upon the success of their advocacy. Accordingly, the professional duties of the adversary attorney consist in zealously defending the client regardless of his or her own interest and view of that client's guilt or innocence and observing strict confidentiality towards all disclosures arising in the lawyer-client relationship.[93]

The Contingent Connection of the Adversary System with Common Law and Trial by Jury

Historically these two prevailing systems of modern trial practice have been tied to two further alternative legal constellations. The inquisitorial system has generally operated with a legal code and comparatively little or no employment of juries, whereas the adversary system has functioned under common law with frequent use of juries. If these connections were essential to each system, they would already tip the balance in behalf of the inquisitorial option. Since due process can be served equally well with or without juries, a predilection for juries is no mark against the adversary system. However, because the universality and objectivity that law ought to give right can only be sufficiently achieved with a legal code, a constitutive tie between common law and adversary practice would weigh in favor of its inquisitorial counter-part.

Are such historical connections, however, really necessary accompaniments of either system? Although inquisitorial systems have been linked with codified law, there is nothing in the common law appeal to judicial precedent that prevents judges from actively directing the impartial fact finding of inquisitorial practice under an uncodified environment. Conversely, the adversary system can unleash its partisan duel just as easily under a legal code as under a tradition of common law. The fact of codification simply does not bear upon whether court procedure restricts lawyers to an objective restraint as handmaidens of the court or sets them loose as adversaries. This issue is a matter of the content of the law of court procedure, rather than a question of the form of law.

Similarly, although adversary partisans might seem to have a more pliable audience for their ploys in a lay jury, courts without juries can prove equally to be an arena for partisan advocacy, as the example of appeal courts in adversary systems can testify. Since judges can be legal experts or lay individuals with legal advisors, any penchant for a lack of legal qualifications on the part of those who judge the facts of the case does not privilege jury trials. Conversely, the inquisitorial system has no necessary incompatibility with jury trials, as exhibited by the limited presence of juries in various legal systems of continental Europe that rely upon inquisitorial trial methods. Whether the facts are uncovered through a contest of partisan adversaries or through a cooperative inquest led by judges, the task of judging what happened remains the same and has the same institutional ramifications.

Consequently, the historical conjunction between, on the one hand, adversary practice, common law, and jury trials, and, on the other hand, inquisitorial practice, codified law, and trial without jury is a contingent fact with no bearing upon the legitimacy of either system. Accordingly, the evaluation of the adversary and inquisitorial systems must address the features of each that are not causally or normatively dependent upon the presence or absence of jury trials and common law.

Many of the distinguishing features of the adversary system have been attributed to the effect of jury trials. The adversary system's emphasis upon placing trial preparation in the hands of the opposing attorneys has been linked by Zweigert and Kötz, for example, to the imperatives of jury trials, which allegedly must operate as continuous oral hearings due to the difficulties of recalling jurors after frequent and lengthy interruptions.[94] Because jury trials proceed as a single hearing, each party must prepare in advance both how to present its own case as well as how to respond to its adversary. Since adjournments cannot be used whenever new evidence and unforeseen arguments are introduced, jury trial lawyers are compelled to interview witnesses in advance and use "discovery" requests to get the opposing party to disclose beforehand any information relevant to the upcoming trial.[95] By contrast, the judge must await the presentations of the opposing attorneys in order to learn what the case involves, leaving them responsible for choosing, ordering, and questioning witnesses, expert or not.[96]

Although these features of the adversary system might well fit the practicalities of convening jurors, they have no special link to those practicalities. An inquisitorial trial could just as easily accommodate the continuous sitting of a jury by having the judge oversee case preparations in advance, including selecting, ordering, and interviewing witnesses before trial, and then taking charge of their questioning in court, leaving lawyers a subsidiary role as impartial aids to the process. Equally, lawyers in an adversary system could still be charged with preparing the case in advance and with selecting, ordering and questioning witnesses during the trial without a jury and without continuous hearings.

Hence, although the relative passivity of the judge in the adversary system may indeed reflect an initial ignorance of the case corresponding to the leading role given to lawyers in preparing and conducting the examination of evidence,[97] none of these features are essentially tied to the practicalities of jury trials. By the same token, the absence of juries has no necessary role in dictating the active function of the judge in the inquisitorial framework, where he or she leads litigants, lawyers, and witnesses to the truth of the case by intervening to overcome their ambiguities, confusions, and mistakes.[98]

Evaluating the Adversary System

The root of these salient differences in procedure must instead be traced back to their normative justification. Since the differences between adversary and inquisitorial systems concern how the first stage of a trial operates, the obvious standard for evaluating them lies in how well they perform the function of uncovering the facts of the case in conformity with due process and the other rights of individuals in civil society.

This standard is customarily employed by advocates of each system. Supporters of the adversary approach typically claim that the free-wheeling duel of partisan lawyers is the best way to discover the truth of the case while upholding the legal rights of litigants. Supporters of the inquisitorial approach equally maintain that subordinating lawyers to the leading role of the judge is the best way to prevent the particular interests of litigants from obstructing an objective discovery of the facts of the case and an impartial enforcement of the rights of all parties to the trial.[99]

Both sides recognize that the demand for uncovering the facts of the case and the demand for upholding the rights of all parties are intertwined. Indeed, in one respect, these two imperatives are identical, for the legal right of individuals to have their rights legally enforced involves the right to have the facts of the case impartially and objectively determined in court. The parting of the ways occurs in identifying the legal procedure that best achieves these imperatives in the first stage of the trial, where the case is prepared for subsumption under the law.

Of course, much legal advocacy involves counseling clients outside of trial proceedings, either to advise them how to employ the law to their own advantage or to advise them how to reach out-of-court settlements and avoid litigation. How lawyers should function in court will naturally affect how their out-of-court counseling should operate. Consequently, although the debate between adversary and inquisitorial systems centers upon how courts can best uphold the rights of individuals and fulfill the imperatives of preparing cases for subsumption under the law, it more broadly extends to the entire lawyer-client relationship.[100]

Admittedly, both the adversary and the inquisitorial systems can be characterized in varying extremes. Some observers, for instance, would identify the adversary system as embodying two principles of legal representation: a principle of partisanship and a principle of nonaccountability.[101] The partisanship principle commits lawyers to acting strictly as advocates of the interest of their client, whereas the principle of nonaccountability sanctions lawyers using any means necessary short of overt crime to promote their client's case.[102] Understood as combining partisanship and nonaccountability, the ethos of the adversary system licenses lawyers to use rules of discovery to harass and overburden their opponent, to call and coach witnesses to commit perjury, to discredit testimony they know is true, to conceal any evidence that might incriminate their client, and to solicit judges and/or jurors biased in their favor.

Can any such version of the adversary system be justified in accord with the rights of civil society? As a normative question, what matters is not that a particular constitution, such as that of the United States, fails to mention the adversary system leaving uncertain whether constitutional guarantees of due process rights mandate an adversary system and whether the adversary system can be supplanted by statute or judicial precedent or only through constitutional amendment.[103] Rather, the determination of whether legal right in civil society mandates adversary practice is what dictates whether particular constitutions warrant revision.

Similarly, the justification of the adversary system cannot rest upon tradition, the fact of its current employment, or the circumstance that it enjoys the consent of legal subjects.[104] An appeal to tradition or current convention is of no avail because normative validity lies not in existence but in conformity with the determination of freedom. Moreover, the fact of consent is not an emblem of legitimacy if the adversary system is itself an impediment to the exercise of rights. The popularity of institutions is no mark of validity if those institutions are themselves obstacles to self-determination. The consent of the governed is not equivalent to the participation of citizenry in democratic self-government. Locke understood this better than his latter-day followers, when he admitted that a civil government could satisfy the liberal requirements of consent and protection of person and property and still take such undemocratic forms as monarchy and oligarchy.[105]

Rationales for the adversary system that escape *these* pitfalls have taken various forms.

Pitfalls of the Adversary System as a Bulwark of Liberty against Public Authority

A familiar argument maintains that zealous partisanship by legal advocates is required to best protect individual liberty from intrusion by public authorities.[106] To be legitimate, this reasoning would have to define individual liberty not in terms of natural right but in terms of the entitlements that individuals enjoy as persons, family members, economic agents, and legal subjects in civil society.

The preceding rationale has been challenged on the ground that it could only apply to criminal cases, where the partisan lawyer faces off against a public prosecutor.[107] That objection does not, however, undermine the appropriateness of the adversary system either for criminal cases or for those civil cases where an individual faces public authorities as party to a suit. After all, the adversary approach need not be mandatory in every type of case for it to be preferable in some.

The relevant question, then, would be whether the adversary system does provide superior protection of the rights of individuals against public authorities, whether they are criminal defendants or civil litigants. Once more, a correct answer requires excluding factors that have no constitutive tie to the adversary-inquisitorial divide.

Due process has already been shown to provide such commonly recognized safeguards of individual rights as the presumption of innocence until proven guilty, the standard of proof that evidence be beyond a reasonable doubt (which should apply in both criminal and civil cases), the prohibition of illegally obtaining evidence,[108] and the requirement that public prosecutors disclose all relevant evidence in a way that allows the accused adequate opportunity to prepare their legal defense. None of these features have any necessary tie to common or codified law, to trial by jury or trial by a panel of judges, or, finally, to an adversary or inquisitorial system. Not one of these protections of right from illegitimate public encroachment depends upon the duel of partisan lawyers for its operation.[109]

Conversely, the practice of plea bargaining, which encourages defendants to forego the full exercise of these protections,[110] has little place in an inquisitorial system, where judges actively ensure that the charges are properly framed and investigated. Admittedly, however, an adversary system could function without plea bargaining[111] and, more fundamentally, without courts allowing guilty pleas to halt the investigation of the facts of a case. Indeed, if an adversary system were to be tolerated, let alone recommended, it would have to operate under that restriction in order to conform to the imperatives of due process. As has been shown, the rights of criminal defendants, victims, and the public all require a proof in court of what happened in every case that comes to trial, confessions notwithstanding.

If none of these bulwarks against public encroachment upon rights is tied to the adversary system, is there any "political argument"[112] left to favor zealous partisanship in court? Properly speaking, the argument is not political, insofar as public authority in the legal system is an institution of civil society, which may just as well be global as national in dimension. Moreover, if the argument revolves around identifying a remedy for protecting individual liberty from the unequal power of public authority, it could well be extended to every situation where individuals go to trial opposing parties able to muster far greater resources, whether corporations, trade unions, consumer groups, religious organizations, or any other influential body in civil society.[113] In that event, the case for the adversary system amounts to the claim that it best protects individuals in court from more forceful opponents, be they public or private institutions, in criminal as well as civil trials.

Yet just as due process protects the legal rights of individuals through the presumption of innocence, the prohibition of improper searches, rules of discovery, and standards of proof, does it not guarantee the right of all litigants to sufficient legal resources without relying upon adversary partisanship? If every legal subject is provided legal aid equal in quality and quantity to any opponent, and if the court guarantees that all evidence is fairly scrutinized, what more is required that a duel of partisans can contribute?

If zealous partisanship enables lawyers successfully to hide incriminating evidence, slander truthful witnesses, and otherwise obstruct the ability of the opposing side to present its case, are not such devices just as readily turned against those who use them to the detriment of their rights? Moreover, when such stratagems work to the advantage of a client, does that not deprive their opponents in civil cases from having their rights duly enforced? And if, in criminal cases, public prosecutors are prohibited to engage in such maneuvres, does not their disadvantage leave both the victims of crime and the public without proper recourse for remedying the infringement of right they suffer? Every crime involves at least a universal wrong against civil society and, when individual victims are involved, a particular wrong warranting restitution or compensation. Consequently, whether a case is civil or criminal, the liberty allegedly protected by adversary methods comes only at the expense of other rights.

Can, however, the adversary system be justified on very different terms, not as the privileged protector of individual liberty from the encroachment of powerful opponents, but rather as the best instrument for securing the constitutive legal aims of every trial, preparing a case for subsumption under the law with proper respect for the rights of all participants? This question has a variety of different dimensions reflecting the concomitant sides of the legal process. Does the adversary system best uncover the truth of a case in court? Alternately, does the adversary system best uphold the rights of due process in effecting the proof of the facts? Or is the adversary system acceptable simply because the inquisitorial alternative is no better on any significant score?

Pitfalls of the Adversary System as a Privileged Instrument of Fact-Finding

Whether an adversary system can best uncover the facts of a case might appear to be an empirical question. If our concern is reaching a normative judgment of truly unconditioned validity, however, what counts is whether any advantages are truly inherent in the adversary approach. Certainly, it would be a mistake to identify the partisan duel of adversary lawyers with the evaluation of competing theories in empirical sciences. Although in both cases the knowledge at issue concerns matters of experience, empirical scientists would hardly claim to be advancing their discipline by knowingly hiding evidence that undermines their theory or discrediting competing experiments they know to be true. If anything, the adoption of an adversary method would be an impediment to scientific progress, since it would license bias and deception in place of an objective scrutiny of all theories in face of all available evidence.[114]

Nor can one assume that the partisan advocacies of opposing parties will reveal all the relevant facts. Either side may well succeed in hiding or discrediting information that deserves to be known, just as disclosures may remain fragmentary and contradictory. Furthermore, there is no guarantee that the complementary distortions and omissions will cancel one another out and somehow leave the unadorned truth. Both sides may offer only deception or incomplete, confusing truths of little use in deciphering the actual facts of the case.[115] It hardly makes sense, then, to maintain that truth is best served when those who dispute the facts are left to do so purely out of concern for their clients' interest, since that interest need neither conform with unveiling the truth, nor balance the interest of trial opponents, and privileging it does not even allow an airing of what each party believes to be true. Whether partisanship will advance the cause of discovery is purely arbitrary. The trial victor is just as likely to be the more successful deceiver as the more successful midwife of truth.[116]

If the sophistry of adversary combat does not better serve proving the facts of a case in court than a disinterested investigation, does it nonetheless best uphold the legal rights of parties to a trial?

Pitfalls of the Adversary System as a Privileged Defender of Legal Rights

Admittedly, the truth-finding function of case preparation does not have unconditioned primacy, as prohibitions against illegal searches indicate.[117] The imperatives of preparing a case for subsumption under the law cannot entail suspending recognition of the property, family, and economic rights of individuals or ignore the rights of due process. To do so would be contradictory, since the whole point of court proceedings is to enforce the legal stipulation of those rights. Hence, any impositions made upon witnesses and other parties to the trial must conform with respecting their other rights and obligations. Granted this proviso, is there any aspect of legal right that requires adversary advocacy for its realization? Is the adversary system a necessary condition for due process or, for that matter, a necessary ingredient of due process, comprising an element of legal right itself?

Adversary lawyers may zealously champion the rights of their respective clients, but why should their complementary advocacies better uphold the rights of either or both parties than a system where lawyers are obliged to defend the rights of their clients and their trial opponents alike?[118] Whereas the success of one adversary lawyer in abusing discovery requests, withholding pertinent information, coaching witnesses, and discrediting true testimony may prevent the opposing party from fulfilling their right to have the facts of the case objectively proven, the success of the opposing adversary lawyer in doing the same may leave the first client in similar straits. In the case of criminal trials where prosecutors have restricted options, the partisan promotion of the rights of the accused may come at the expense of those of victim and public alike. The impartial umpiring of trial judges cannot remove these likelihoods when adversary lawyers execute trial preparation and the selection and scrutiny of evidence. Far from offering a self-checking system in protection of legal rights, the adversary duel presents a trial framework where opposing lawyers can no more be counted upon to check each other's failure to uphold the rights of clients, victims, or the public than presiding judges can be relied upon to check them both.[119] This predicament could be tolerated solely if the defense of rights in court could not avoid jeopardizing the client's very own rights and/or those of others. But must legal rights be condemned to a morass of self-contradiction?

Pitfalls of the Adversary System as a Necessary Ingredient in the Recognition of the Dignity of Legal Subjects

Even if the adversary system cannot guarantee the legal rights of individuals, does it warrant acceptance as part of how the legal process must respect the dignity of legal subjects? As a responsible agent before the law, each legal subject deserves to be treated as innocent until proven guilty and therefore to be considered to be arguing in good faith when pressing charges, responding to accusations, or otherwise testifying. Does this right not entail that parties should have their cases presented in court by partisans of their position, rather than submitting to an impartial investigation conducted by public judicial officials?[120]

At best, such considerations dictate only that parties to a trial be entitled to have their positions presented in court and considered as good faith positions until the examination of evidence is judged to prove otherwise. This entitlement, which is an element of legal subjects' right to have the facts of their case objectively investigated in court, can be satisfied just as well in an inquisitorial trial where judges solicit testimony from the parties as in an adversary duel. Moreover, judging parties to have advanced their legal claims in good faith by no means grants them license to withhold or distort evidence or to tarnish the veridical testimony of others.[121] Toleration of these prerogatives of an adversary system instead amounts to withdrawing respect for the good faith of those they are directed against.[122]

The Remedy of the Inquisitorial System

The adversary system has proven to be neither a privileged instrument of fact-finding or a privileged protector of legal rights. Does it nonetheless still warrant acceptance, at least by current users, as David Luban urges, because no alternative is any better on either score, some trial system is required, and the expense of replacement is not worth the bother?[123]

This pragmatic argument hinges upon the denial that the inquisitorial system has a normative edge in bringing a case to the point of subsumption under the law. Are the adversary and inquisitorial systems indeed, however, indifferent alternatives with regard to legal right?

Each system must be compared in the context of what law in civil society prescribes for the legal process. As we have seen, right mandates that law be codified but leaves open the question of whether trials should employ juries. Accordingly, although inquisitorial systems have usually appeared in conjunction with codified law and without jury trials, whereas adversary systems have operated under common law and trial by jury, both must be judged in respect to how they function with legal codification[124] and with or without jury trials.

Under these conditions, is the inquisitorial system better at fulfilling the fact-finding function of trials and at upholding the rights of individuals in court? What must decide the issue are the ramifications of the distinguishing features of the inquisitorial system: the generally expanded role of judges in preparing and conducting the trial, and the relatively nonpartisan, subsidiary role of lawyers.

In an inquisitorial trial, judges first study dossiers presented by prosecutors or civil litigants and their representatives. On this basis, judges then determine the order of the introduction and examination of evidence, deciding whether witnesses and material exhibits selected by the trial parties need to be supplemented and determining if expert witnesses need to testify and choosing who they will be. Judges proceed to question witnesses, who are not permitted to be coached by lawyers of the parties to the trial.

Other features have been historically associated with inquisitorial trials that are actually mandated by due process and could just as well be incorporated in adversary systems without removing their distinctive traits. First, all duly prepared cases are tried without permitting guilty pleas to abort the trial fact-finding. In other words, avowals of guilt are treated simply as matters of evidence on a par with any other testimony. Second, when judges decide that the evidence calls for altering the charges, they are empowered to reformulate them[125] and redirect the trial accordingly.[126]

More essential to the verdict on inquisitorial trials are the features that distinguish the role of lawyers under its system. In inquisitorial trials, lawyers operate not as partisan advocates of particular parties to a trial but more as occupants of a public office, charged with assisting individuals to exercise their rights before the court.[127] Accordingly, whatever remuneration they receive cannot be tied to the victory of their party, and their professional ethics do not give them license to withhold evidence or harass opponents by manipulating rules of discovery.

This nonpartisan role is reflected in the tradition of inquisitorial practices in France, where until 1957 the *avocat* could not sue a client for fees but received at most an honorarium.[128] Although French lawyers now have a contractual monetary relation to those they represent, this shift has not canceled their professional role as public servants, responsible to the court.[129]

In this capacity as impartial aids to an official inquiry, inquisitorial trial lawyers nominate witnesses and select material exhibits but observe strict guidelines in avoiding any contact that might prejudice testimony and evidence. During the trial, lawyers may question witnesses in court to supplement their examination by judges, but in so doing, lawyers remain subordinate to the judges, who exercise final say in how the examination of the facts will be conducted.

In several key respects, these distinguishing roles of inquisitorial judge and lawyer overcome basic lacuna in the adversary system's proof of the facts of a case. As we have seen, the duel of partisan lawyers cannot itself be counted upon to present the whole truth and nothing but the truth. The coaching of witnesses can easily hinder rather than promote genuine fact-finding. Moreover, contingency fees can further spur lawyers to advance their client's case at the expense of truth, the rights of opponents to due compensation, and the rights of civil society to due punishment of malefactors. Coaching of witnesses and contingency fees could conceivably be banned while retaining other aspects of the adversary system, just as restrictions upon lawyer-client confidentiality could limit the ability of adversary lawyers to withhold incriminating evidence without canceling their partisan duel. However, none of these sanitizing measures can solve the problem when adversary lawyers retain the sole prerogative of selecting and examining witnesses and material exhibits.

The inquisitorial system overcomes these limitations not only by eliminating the coaching of witnesses and limiting lawyer-client confidentiality but by empowering judges to call supplementary witnesses and to raise the questions that lawyers have wrongfully ignored. In these ways, the inquisitorial system frees the trial's fact-finding from overbearing dependence upon the efforts of partisan lawyers. Moreover, the inquisitorial system does so without excluding lawyers from playing a supplementary role to counteract shortcomings in the judge's leading of the inquiry. Although inquisitorial procedure lets judges chiefly decide what evidence is considered and what queries are put to witnesses, this provision does not sacrifice fact-finding and trial rights at the altar of judicial license.[130] Lawyers are and should be able to nominate witnesses and material exhibits and to engage in additional questioning whenever judges have overlooked areas of inquiry. In this way, they can function as impartial guardians of trial justice, fulfilling their professional ethic to be as independent of judges as of their client.[131] A properly functioning inquisitorial system, then, provides for checking the efforts of judge and lawyer alike.

Since the rights of parties to a trial hang in the balance when fact-finding is improperly conducted, the foregoing achievements equally confer preeminence upon the inquisitorial system as a protector of legal rights, assuming that it operates in conformity with the other guidelines of due process.

Are there any grounds, however, for questioning the ability of the inquisitorial framework from upholding these other dimensions of trial rights? One might be tempted to argue that without contingency fees clients without means will not be able to protect their rights in civil suits. If public authorities fulfill their duty to provide all legal subjects with adequate legal resources in *both* criminal and civil cases, however, this problem would never arise. Moreover, if this guarantee is accompanied by public imposition of fixed legal fees, such as currently practiced in the inquisitorial systems of France[132] and Germany, both the affordability and the impartiality of lawyers can be promoted.[133] Admittedly, operating a system of legal aid may demand that undeserving suits be winnowed out to keep litigation from exploding beyond the means of civil society to provide legal service for all. However, this problem, which has its analogues in the obligation of civil society to provide its members with adequate health care, food, clothing, and shelter, as well as adequate family care and economic opportunity, follows from basic imperatives of legal right that apply whether or not inquisitorial or adversary systems are embraced. To abandon the guarantee of legal aid because of the eventuality of administrative screening would jeopardize every legal right of individuals, since each can be violated nonmaliciously and warrant being brought to court as a civil case. Moreover, such screening by no means vests a dangerous degree of power in the judiciary.[134] Not only could appeal procedures be instituted to check initial screenings, but accountability could be fostered by the same methods of selection and regulation of judicial positions that reign in judicial abuse in the courtroom.

Further, can one not object, on the one hand, that because inquisitorial trial judges depend upon prosecutors' dossiers to organize the hearing of evidence in criminal cases, their independence is undercut and the trial becomes reduced to a formal replay of pretrial investigations?[135] This dependence, however, is hardly absolute. Judges have the power to revise both the charges and the roll of witnesses and material exhibits at any time the trial's fact-finding requires. Moreover, lawyers can use their prerogative to call additional witnesses and introduce other material exhibits.[136] Consequently, judges and lawyers alike can insure that prosecutors have no more privileged a role in an inquisitorial trial than they have in an adversary trial.

On the other hand, do not inquisitorial trials of civil cases exclude the use of juries and thereby further enhance a risky dependency upon the integrity of judges? The absence of juries might seem mandated by the fact that inquisitorial judges must interrupt trial proceedings after opposing litigants present their positions in order to study them. These interruptions might then make it unfeasible to maintain a jury, whose members would be intermittently forced to withdraw from their everyday commitments.[137] It certainly can be questioned whether inquisitorial trials of civil offenses require either more frequent and lengthy adjournments than occur in adversary trials, as well as whether arrangements cannot be made to impanel a jury, with due compensation for whatever disruptions occur through court recesses. Once more, the connection between jury trials and inquisitorial or adversary systems proves to be contingent. Moreover, even if an iron rule of practicality precluded jury trials in inquisitorial civil cases, one could still question the alleged primacy of jury trials as a bulwark against dangerous entrusting of judges. This alleged primacy is directly challenged by all the previous arguments against privileging jury trials. Not only are the integrity and impartiality of jurors no more reliable than those of judges, but the alternative ways of staffing and regulating judicial positions allows for various checks upon judicial accountability. Jury trials are hardly the only, let alone the most effective, means of enabling community control to reign in abuses in the legal system. Moreover, the appeal process provides a further means for upholding due impartiality, whether a trial employs jurors or not.

Similarly, one might suspect that allowing judges to select expert witnesses and lead questioning places too much trust in the integrity and competence of the judiciary.[138] Once again, this concern can be mitigated on two complementary grounds. First, inquisitorial judges can be held accountable through appeals as well as by selection, promotion, and dismissal procedures and other administrative monitoring. Secondly, an inquisitorial trial can still give lawyers the opportunity to question witnesses and nominate witnesses of their own. Moreover, a reliance upon coached partisan expert witnesses hardly guarantees a fairer hearing of the truth.

Although judges in contemporary inquisitorial systems may be life-tenured members of the civil service, instead of being directly elected or appointed by elected officials as in the U.S. adversary system, this fact does not signify that inquisitorial practice demands trust, let alone an unfounded trust, in bureaucratic elites.[139] Neither mode of becoming a judge is incompatible with the inquisitorial system. Further, even if inquisitorial judges were civil servants, judicial appeal, the self-policing of the bureaucracy, or democratic government's supervision of the civil service could still check possible judicial abuses.

On all these counts, the inquisitorial system hardly comprises an obstacle to legitimate popular control of the judicial process,[140] let alone a foe of trial justice and the upholding of rights in civil society. On the contrary, by bringing cases to the point of subsumption under the law with the most impartial, objective investigation of the facts and the most thorough maintenance of legal right, the inquisitorial trial stands in clear advance of its adversary counterpart.[141] They are not normatively indifferent options, to be selected on solely pragmatic grounds. Legal right is better served by the inquisitorial system, and any legal order that tolerates the adversary alternative perpetrates an injustice.[142]

Implementation of the Verdict

Once the court verdict has been laid down and weathered subsequent appeals, it takes immediate effect. Those whose rights have been violated must now be provided with due compensation, either by those responsible for their losses or by public authority, whereas whomever has been judged to have committed a crime must be subjected to due punishment.

Both of these aspects of the enforcement of court verdicts must be publicly performed according to lawful regulations that are themselves subject to legal enforcement. No matter what role litigants may be judged to have played in the case, they all remain legal subjects, fully entitled to every right to which a member of civil society is endowed. Since to have a right is to possess an entitlement against others to which they are equally entitled, the duty of all parties to fulfill their obligations to others is part and parcel of the recognition of their own rights. Consequently, when defendants are required to compensate victims and endure punishment, they are not deprived of any rights. On the contrary, to hold them responsible in this fashion is precisely what respect for their right mandates, for only those who have corresponding rights can be held accountable for respecting the same rights of others. Liberal theorists from Hobbes to Kant[143] are therefore far off the mark in maintaining that criminals have forfeited their right and dignity, and that, thereby being cast out of civil society and back into a state of nature, they are no longer obliged to endure punishment but face penal authorities as combatants in a war of all against all.[144]

A similar neglect for the right of criminals is committed by penal authorities who view their function as one of reforming their charges and who therefore treat good behavior in prison as a sign of rehabilitation warranting reduction of sentences and parole. Although parole may serve to maintain order in prisons, any attempt to tie it to rehabilitation is tantamount to treating prisoners as less than fully responsible. If in fact they are not responsible, they should be judged unfit to have stood trial and received punishment in the first place.

Since criminals have been convicted of acting consciously against the law with the ability and opportunity to know what is legal, due punishment consists in striking at their will in its opposition to right. Incarceration is therefore the fitting penal instrument, since it restricts criminals' capacity to act for an appropriate term, without otherwise undermining their dignity. Punishments that rely instead upon inflicting physical pain and mutilation treat individuals like animals, for whom only the compulsions of pain and pleasure, but not the restriction of the will, can be the issue. Similarly, punishments that condemn criminals to servitude under a private master[145] equally violate the abiding right of the convicted to be recognized as a person, subject only to public restraint.

We must not forget that the will that deserves restriction is the criminal's arbitrary will, not the willing that is in accord with right. Accordingly, prisoners should not be deprived of any of their entitlements as members of civil society over and above the restrictions imposed by incarceration and responsibility for compensation to victims. Convicts retain their right to property, their rights as parent and spouse, their economic rights, their due process rights, and, by way of anticipation, their political rights. Insofar as upholding each of these rights may require going to court, prisoners should be afforded whatever legal assistance they require.

The Abiding Political Dimension of Law

Law in civil society reaches the end of its process with the settling of cases, compensating victims and punishing offenders. Law, however, has a further reality extending beyond civil relations in two basic respects.

First, domestic political institutions refashion legality in conformity with the freedoms of self-government. This development introduces constitutionality and the branches of government that legislate, authorize, and execute statutory law. The legal code accordingly expands. On the one hand, codification extends to laws that prescribe legitimate political conduct in and out of office and prohibit violations of political rights, which now rest upon drawing a legal distinction between citizens and noncitizens and defining legal jurisdiction in terms of political boundaries. On the other hand, the legal code internalizes the divide between statutory and constitutional law, which extends beyond directly political affairs to every sphere of right that law can enforce. For its part, the legal process, from courts to penal institutions, now operates in respect to both the expanded legal code and the political supervision that undergirds legality with a new seat of power and authority.[146]

Second, the plurality of states gives rise to an international law that not only has the global dimension of civil society but contains the concrete differentiation of individual body politics. Although this law gives international scope to the rights of civil society, it now must extend to the rights of self-government and the due relations of states to one another.[147]

These dimensions of law can only be determined in conjunction with conceiving the institutions of political freedom. The conception of law in civil society may not completely prescribe what law should be, but it does set the stage for tackling this frontier of political justice, within which law receives its ultimate determination.

Notes

Introduction: Law and Freedom

1. In drawing these distinctions, I am following Norberto Bobbio in his essay, "The Rule of Men or the Rule of Law," in Bobbio, *The Future of Democracy*, trans. Roger Griffin (Minneapolis: University of Minnesota Press, 1987), 138–156.

2. Ibid., 141.

3. Ibid., 143.

4. Ibid.

5. Ibid., 144.

6. Ibid.

7. Michael Oakeshott emphasizes this point; see Oakeshott, *On Human Conduct* (Oxford: Oxford University Press, 1975), 126, 130.

8. Ibid., 144.

9. Ibid.

10. This requirement provides one of the chief rationales for respecting the authority of judicial precedent, in whose absence, it could be argued, the mere promulgation of standing laws provides no guarantee of what they actually will signify in practice.

11. John Rawls, *A Theory of Justice* (Cambridge: Harvard University Press, 1971), 239.

12. Michael B. Foster, *The Political Philosophies of Plato and Hegel* (Oxford: Oxford University Press, 1968), 113–116.

13. Ibid., 116.

14. Oakeshott, *On Human Conduct*, 126, 130.

15. Foster, *Political Philosophies*, 121.

16. Bobbio, *Future of Democracy*, 145.

17. Ibid.

18. Ibid., 146.

19. Foster regards this connection between economic freedom and rule by law as inherent in the generality of law. Yet the fact that law does not specify

the full detail of the activities by which it is obeyed does not of itself provide the specific prerogatives of market freedom on which economic laws depend. See Foster, *Political Philosophies*, 129–130.

20. Hegel's *Philosophy of Right* provides a central contribution to this endeavor, both because it conceives justice as the reality of self-determination and because it attempts to situate law with due attention to the different institutions of freedom. Yet Hegel's treatment of law has received relatively little attention—partly because of the brevity of Hegel's analysis of legal institutions, located in the section entitled "The Administration of Justice," and partly because of the greater allure of his treatment of the other institutions of civil society and the state. Nevertheless, Hegel's discussion of legality raises the issues that become most acute when normativity is identified with freedom and the value of law is called into question. Moreover, Hegel's conception of law is embedded within an ethical theory that, once properly reconstructed, provides the tools for overcoming the dilemmas of foundationalism that have plagued his predecessors and successors in ethics. For these reasons, a critical encounter with Hegel's conception of law is a worthy point of departure for reconceiving what law should be.

Chapter 1. The Normativity of Freedom

1. This chapter incorporates, with some modifications and additions, my article "Freedom from Foundations: The Normativity of Autonomy in Theory and Practice" published in the *Jadavpur Journal of Philosophy*, 4:1 (Fall 1992): 1–27.

2. For a more detailed exploration and critique of these strategies, see Richard Dien Winfield, *Reason and Justice* (Albany: State University of New York Press, 1988), pts. 1–3, 19–155.

3. Although, taking the example of Kant, one might be tempted to argue that the knowledge in question is only a priori objective knowledge and that empirical knowledge can be obtained by relying upon the individual matter of experience, knowledge of that material side of experience remains subject to irremovable doubts that can only be bracketed out by pragmatic agreement to accept a certain level of trust in observation, whose results must still always remain corrigible beliefs.

4. So it is that Kant, who offers his three critiques as preliminaries to a further metaphysics, ends up determining what is essential to nature, ethics and beauty in these critiques, adding only analytic extrapolations upon their doctrines in his subsequent *Metaphysical Foundations of Natural Science* and *Metaphysics of Morals*.

5. For further critique of these avenues of transcendental argument, see Richard Dien Winfield, *Overcoming Foundations: Studies in Systematic Philosophy* (New York: Columbia University Press, 1989), 16–19, 41–45, 61–64, 91–98, 99–116; Winfield, *Freedom and Modernity* (Albany: State University of New York Press, 1991), 15–18; and Winfield, "Hegel's Remedy for

the Impasse of Contemporary Philosophy," *Reason Papers* 16 (Fall 1991): 115–119.

6. For further analogous critiques of post-modernism, see Carl Rapp, "Coming out into the Corridor: Post-Modern Phantasies of Pluralism," *Georgia Review* 41:3 (Fall 1987): 533–553; Carl Rapp, "The Crisis of Reason in Contemporary Thought: Some Reflections on the Arguments of Post-Modernism," *Critical Review* 5:2 (Spring 1991): 261–290; and William Maker, *Philosophy without Foundations: Rethinking Hegel* (Albany: State University of New York Press, 1994).

7. For a detailed development of how determinacy is accounted for, see Winfield, *Overcoming Foundations*, 55–75.

8. For this reason, Hegel identifies the first part of his foundation-free systematic philosophy as *The Science of Logic*.

9. For a further discussion of how the science of logic converges with the self-development of self-determined determinacy, see Winfield, *Freedom and Modernity*, 3–13.

Chapter 2. The System of Right as the Frame of Law

1. The following discussions reconstruct and revise arguments in Hegel's *Philosophy of Right*. For a more comprehensive account of these spheres of right, see Richard Dien Winfield, *Reason and Justice*, (Albany: State University of New York Press, 1988), pt. 3; Winfield, *The Just Economy* (New York: Routledge, 1988), pt. 2; Winfield, *Overcoming Foundations: Studies in Systematic Philosophy* (New York: Columbia University Press, 1989), pt. 2; and Winfield, *Freedom and Modernity*, (Albany: State University of New York Press, 1991), pt. 2.

2. Although Hobbes allows for covenant and the formation of civil society and its body politic prior to the establishment of property relations by the sovereign, he does acknowledge the priority of property to distributive justice, observing how, in "that *justice is the constant will of giving to every man his own* . . . therefore where there is no *own*, that is no propriety, there is no injustice" (Thomas Hobbes, *Leviathan* [Harmondsworth, Eng.: Penguin Books, 1968], chap. 15, 473).

3. Kant ends up following in Hobbes's footsteps, for although Kant conceives of property right prior to the contractual enactment of a civil condition, such property right remains merely provisional, echoing Hobbes's judgment that there can be no mine and thine prior to the foundation of a commonwealth. See, respectively, Immanuel Kant, *The Metaphysics of Morals*, trans. Mary Gregor (New York: Cambridge University Press, 1991), sec. 15, 85 ff., Ak. 264–266; and Hobbes, *Leviathan*, chap. 13, 183–188, and chap. 15, 473.

4. An analogous blunder is committed by thinkers such as Stephen Munzer, who distinguish moral from legal property rights, not realizing that property has a normativity of its own distinct from both moral accountability

and legal right (Stephen R. Munzer, *A Theory of Property* [New York: Cambridge University Press, 1990], 39.)

5. Consequently, right-based arguments are not primarily concerned with the promotion of an individual interest, as Jeremy Waldron maintains, following Mill's lead. (Waldron, *The Right to Private Property* [Oxford: Oxford University Press, 1988], 347.) Right instead fundamentally concerns the realization of freedom, which, in the first instance of property right, involves no reference to interests, be they individual or communal. Accordingly, contra Waldron, the embodiment of a person's will in property has in itself no reference to any further practical possibilities that that ownership provides. (ibid., 372–373).

6. Ernest J. Weinrib's "Right and Advantage in Private Law" argues this point at length in his critique of Nozick's proviso on appropriation. See *Cardozo Law Review*, 10:5–6 (March/April 1989): 1293–1297.

7. Waldron, *Right to Private Property*, 177–183.

8. Although Marx overcomes this oversight in *Capital*, where his labor theory of value rests upon differentiating labor and labor power, Waldron et al. do not (see Waldron, *Right to Private Property*, 378, 380).

9. Kant makes this suggestion in *The Metaphysics of Morals*, trans. Mary Gregor (New York: Cambridge University Press, 1991), 90, Ak. 270, although he otherwise fails to mention ownership of one's body, let alone its priority.

10. Alan Brudner ignores this constitutive intersubjectivity of the right to self-ownership when he claims that it is established without relation to others. See Alan Brudner, *Unity of the Common Law* (Berkeley: University of California Press, 1994), chap. 4, sec. 3.1.

11. See Winfield, *Reason and Justice*, 173–174, for a further discussion of the solution to the seeming vicious circularity of self-ownership.

12. Munzer, *Theory of Property*, 37, 41–44.

13. Ibid., 50.

14. Ibid., 37, 48–56.

15. Contrary to Kant, self-ownership and not ownership of land is the ultimate condition making possible ownership of external objects. See Kant, *Metaphysics of Morals*, 83, Ak. 261; 134, Ak. 323.

16. Munzer, *Theory of Property*, 38, 56–58.

17. Entitled ownership is thus hardly constituted by any monological relation, such as making a factor and being in a position to use and further modify it, as Waldron erroneously suggests in interpreting Hegel's account of property (Waldron, *Right to Private Property*, 369). Unless an agent wills in respect to the willing of others, no relation of right and duty comes into play, and no genuine self-determination occurs, whereby agents succeed in determining the form and content of their own agency (see Winfield, *Reason and Justice*, 160–165).

18. This first occupancy by no means requires any assumption that redistribution of property is impossible, as Waldron maintains (Waldron, *Right to Private Property*, 389). On the contrary, other spheres of right, such as those

of family, social, and political right, will realize freedoms that impose partial redistributions of property without undermining the general right of personhood, including the right to first occupancy, on which their own freedoms depend.

19. For a discussion of this point and its ramifications for how tort law should treat nuisance, see Weinrib, "Right and Advantage in Private Law," 1283–1309.

20. Waldron misses this basic point in maintaining that Hegel does not show how "*alienable* property is needed in order for humans to be free persons" (Waldron, *Right to Private Property*, 369).

21. Kant is therefore mistaken in claiming that when a contract is agreed upon the parties obtain only a right to the acts comprising the performance of the contract, but do not obtain a right to the properties whose ownership changes until the stipulated contract terms are executed. Indeed, Kant's reliance upon physical possession here contradicts his own emphasis upon the noumenal, as opposed to physical character of ownership. See Kant, *Metaphysics of Morals*, 94–95, para. 21, Ak. 275–276.

22. For a critique of Peter Benson's claim that market price should govern the equivalencies of value in contract, see Richard Dien Winfield, "With What Must Ethics Begin? Reflections on Benson's Account of Property and Contract," *Cardozo Law Review* 11:3 (February 1990): 546–547, and Alan Brudner, "Hegel and the Crisis of Private Law," *Cardozo Law Review* 10:5–6, (March/April 1989): 996, ftn. 138.

23. This principle, however, lacks rationality when it comes to determining liability for nonmalicious wrongs, as will be shown in the next section.

24. Winfield, "With What Must Ethics Begin?" 545–548.

25. Roberto Mangabeira Unger, *The Critical Legal Studies Movement* (Cambridge: Harvard University Press, 1986), 6off.

26. See Joel Feinberg, *Harm to Others*, vol. 1 of *The Moral Limits of the Criminal Law* (New York: Oxford University Press, 1984), 31ff.

27. In his article "Right and Advantage In Private Law," 1283 ff., Weinrib discusses such an example, showing just how property right and wrong are independent of benefit and disadvantage.

28. Although Hegel is perhaps the first philosopher to properly draw the distinction between nonmalicious and malicious wrongs, he tends to ignore unintended injuries as a result of behavior or effects of property, focusing upon disagreements in interpretations of property entitlements when identifying nonmalicious wrong.

29. Robert Berman has pointed this out in conversation.

30. Aristotle draws this distinction well in his *Nicomachean Ethics*, bk. 3, even though his discussion of corrective justice, which accounts for compensation of injuries and losses, provides no justification for punishment.

31. As with negligent and openly criminal activity, what makes bad Samaritan omissions punishable is not that we have intuitions supporting such punishment, as Joel Feinberg argues in defending the criminalization of bad Samaritan behavior (see Feinberg, *Harm to Others*, 128), but rather that

person and property are maliciously harmed in such a case according to the concept of property right. Even if legality is an institution of ethical community, where the authority of law is tied to its efficacy, which is grounded in a certain degree of recognition, one cannot appeal to given intuitions to determine what limits crime or any other normatively relevant matter should have. All such appeals, commonly followed under the banner of "reflective equilibrium," either resuscitate the foundational dilemmas plaguing the metaphysical appeal to the given or revert to a nihilism for which all intuitions are arbitrary and no intuition can have primacy over any other.

32. As Peter P. Nicholson points out in his essay "Hegel On Crime," (*History of Political Thought* 3:1, [Spring-January 1982]: 120), this feature of malicious wrong allows for victimless crimes. However, that such victimless crimes comprise not just attempted harm to the person and property of others but completed acts that maliciously violate right without ever having any victims involves applying the category of malicious wrong beyond the sphere of property right into the more concrete concerns of civil society, where drug use and the like might be prohibited.

33. Ernest J. Weinrib, "The Case for a Duty to Rescue," *Yale Law Journal*, 90:2 (December 1980): 256.

34. Weinrib has effectively argued this point in "Right and Advantage in Private Law," 1304–1308, although he thereby excludes strict liability from Abstract Right, ignoring how liability for compensating nonmalicious wrong is a case of strict liability falling within property relations.

35. This welfare consideration can only apply in reference to the more concrete rights pertaining to membership in the family, civil society, and the state. Accordingly, criminal negligence can take on a wider scope when the rights of these spheres come into play, just as malicious wrong in general can then be extended to cover intentional violations of the family, civil, and political rights of individuals.

36. Although Alan Brudner correctly suggests that legal institutions end up aiming at upholding an effective autonomy of legal subjects that extends beyond the formal limits of property right, he wrongly denies that negligence is still initially defined in terms of property right without involving the more concrete rights of need and welfare that family association and civil society introduce. See Brudner, *Unity of the Common Law*, chap. 4, sec. 2.1.

37. This outcome is reflected in the traditional negligence tort law, which denies recovery of damages for negligence without injury but otherwise ties damage awards to the plaintiff's injury. Ernest J. Weinrib discusses these points in his article "Causation and Wrongdoing," (*Chicago-Kent Law Review*, 63:3, [1987]: 448–449), without, however, focusing upon the element of general wrong rendering negligence *criminal* and subject to punishment.

38. The risk in question refers only to jeopardizing person and property and not to wider matters of convenience and welfare, whose claims count only in further spheres of right. For this reason, Ernest Weinrib's argument for the duty to rescue on the Kantian terms of personhood and a kingdom of ends is too broad, even though the thrust of the argument can readily fit within

the more narrow confines of property right. See Weinrib, "Case for a Duty to Rescue," 287–290.

39. Hegel discusses the right of necessity *(Notrecht)* within his analysis of morality, which seems to suggest that he considers any duty to rescue to be moral in character rather than an obligation of property right. See the *Philosophy of Right*, para. 127.

40. Employing a Kantian moral framework, Weinrib suggests that the duty to rescue applies only to emergencies where the life of the victim is imperiled, with the caveat that rescuers not suffer inconveniences that radically interfere with their coherent pursuit of their own chosen ends. ("Case for a Duty to Rescue," 289.) This qualification does not apply to property right, for which the only mitigating factor would be a threat to the person of the rescuer, something not at all identical with a threat to a chosen life plan.

41. For a recent example of such a defense of the duty to rescue, see Feinberg, *Harm to Others*, 126–186.

42. Weinrib, "Case for a Duty to Rescue," 249, 280–281. As we have seen, the rule against liability for nonfeasance only applies when nonmalicious wrong is not involved.

43. Alan Brudner falsely assumes that a contradiction is here unavoidable within the framework of formalist tort law, ignoring that what lies at stake is not a duty to care for particular interests going beyond the right of owners, but rather the duty to uphold personhood itself, even when doing so involves *particular* impositions upon the property of others. See Brudner, *Unity of the Common Law*, chap. 4, sec. 2.3.

44. Ernest Weinrib makes these points in Kantian terms in "Case for a Duty to Rescue," 292.

45. Thus, as Hegel suggests, in civil society, the threat a crime represents to the fabric of society will enter into determining the type and magnitude of the punishment, but the decision about whether someone should be punished remains dependent upon guilt, since doing otherwise would undermine recognition of the autonomy of persons, without which no further relations of right can be sustained (see Hegel, *Philosophy of Right*, para. 218).

46. The analysis of moral freedom that follows draws upon Hegel's account of morality in the *Philosophy of Right*. For a more detailed reconstruction and evaluation of Hegel's account, see Winfield, *Overcoming Foundations*, chap. 8, "The Limits of Morality," 135–170, and Winfield, *Freedom and Modernity*, chap. 6, "Morality without Community," 61–75.

47. See Winfield, *Freedom and Modernity*, 70–71.

48. Thus Hegel describes the love ingredient in the ethical association of marriage. See Hegel, *Philosophy of Right*, para. 163.

49. All the foregoing features of the relationship between spouses in a free family can apply not only to marriages of two partners but conceivably to marriages involving more individuals, no matter what the combination of gender and sexual orientation. Although, historically, polygamous and polyandrous marriages have generally failed to meet the standards of freedom and mutual authority required for normative validity in relations among spouses,

the same can be said of the historical monogamous marriage. For a further discussion of these issues, see Winfield, *Reason and Justice,* 188–189.

50. That the market is a structure of ethical community has been equally ignored by liberal theorists of justice, marginal utility economists (who rely upon psychological models), and rational choice theorists.

51. For further discussions of the anatomy of this system, see David P. Levine, *Economic Theory* vols. 1 and 2 (London: Routledge and Kegan Paul, 1978, 1981), and Winfield, *Just Economy.*

52. Unger is mistaken in equating a regime of contract with the market (Unger, *Critical Legal Studies Movement,* 67), for just as property is not identical with the commodity (not all property can take the commodity form, although all commodities are property), so commercial transactions are subject to imperatives of equal economic opportunity that are not contained in the norms of contract mandated by property right. For this very reason, in civil society, the right of contract gets modified, as Unger himself notes (67), in accord with such social provisos as that economically unfair bargains not be enforced.

53. Habermas makes this bogus claim (see Jürgen Habermas, *Legitimationsprobleme im Spätkapitalismus* [Frankfurt am Main: Suhrkamp, 1973]) in conformity with his communicative ethics, which, like all versions of liberal social contract theory, cannot make sense of ethical community and the concrete rights it involves. A similar inability marks the controversy in feminist theory between advocates of rights (understood in the formal terms of liberal theory) and advocates of care. Once again, the rigid separation rests upon a failure to conceive of ethical community as a structure of freedom.

Chapter 3. Civil Society as the Arena of Legality

1. For a detailed discussion of the contrast between morality and ethical community, see "The Limits of Morality," chap. 8 in Winfield, *Overcoming Foundations: Studies in Systematic Philosophy* (New York: Columbia University Press, 1989), 135–170, and "Morality without Community," chap. 6 in Winfield, *Freedom and Modernity* (Albany: State University of New York Press, 1991), 61–75.

2. So, for instance, the inability of civil law to guarantee the equal economic opportunity of the individuals whose property it protects will enter into determining what a public administration of welfare must do to regulate the market and how the body of law must be expanded to complement the enforcement of property and family rights with an enforcement of economic right. For a further discussion of this point, see Winfield, *The Just Economy* (New York: Routledge, 1988), 175ff.

3. G. W. F. Hegel, *Vorlesungen über Rechtsphilosophie,* ed. Ilting (Stuttgart–Bad Cannstatt: Frommann-Holzboog, 1974), 3:642.

4. Michael Oakeshott emphasizes this aspect of law in *On Human Conduct,* (Oxford: Oxford University Press, 1975), 128ff.

5. Hegel, *Vorlesungen über Rechtsphilosophie*, 3:642–643.

6. Ibid., 643.

7. Like most communitarian thinkers, Roberto Mangabeira Unger identifies ethical community with an association united in the recognition of common particular aims (see Roberto Mangabeira Unger, *Law in Modern Society: Towards a Criticism of Social Theory* [New York: Free Press, 1976], 30 ff.). This identification makes it difficult to conceive legality as a form of ethical community, since law in civil society leaves largely undetermined what ends can be pursued within the law. To the degree that legality is instead concerned with positing right, legality escapes the difficulties plaguing the heteronomous account of ethical community as an association in pursuit of shared particular values.

8. Hegel, *Vorlesungen über Rechtsphilosophie*, 4:533.

9. Hegel, *Vorlesungen über Rechtsphilosophie*, 3:643.

10. The Marxist legal theorist Pashukanis analogously upholds this enabling fit between commodity relations and legality. However, due to his orthodox view of markets as transient historical formations bereft of any universal validity, Pashukanis is left to conclude that the communist overcoming of commodity relations will carry with it the withering away of legality, thereby eliminating any place for a genuinely normative legal theory. See Evgeny B. Pashukanis, *Law and Marxism: A General Theory*, trans. Barbara Einhorn (London: Ink Links, 1978), 58ff.

11. Hegel, *Vorlesungen über Rechtsphilosophie*, 4:531.

12. Karl Marx, *Capital* (New York: International Publishers, 1968), 1:585.

13. Karl Marx, *Early Writings*, trans. T. B. Bottomore (New York: McGraw-Hill, 1964), 29–30.

14. That the positing of law need not be statutory and parasitic upon political relations is indicated by common law and judicial precedent, even if neither affords legality a fully adequate form.

15. Aristotle, *Nicomachean Ethics*, bk. 5, chap. 7, 1134b–1135a.

16. Hobbes, *Leviathan*, chap. 21, "Of the Liberty of Subjects," 261ff.

17. Michael Foster mistakenly criticizes Hegel for allegedly embracing this overly Platonic conception of the positivity of legality. See M. B. Foster, *The Political Philosophies of Plato and Hegel* (Oxford: Oxford University Press, 1968), 117–121.

18. G. W. F. Hegel, *Philosophy of Right*, trans. T. M. Knox (New York: Oxford University Press, 1967), para. 210; Hegel, *Vorlesungen über Rechtsphilosophie*, 3:644; 4:533.

Chapter 4. Law as the Promulgation of Right

1. G. W. F. Hegel, *Philosophy of Right*, trans. T. M. Knox (New York: Oxford University Press, 1967), para. 211.

2. G. W. F. Hegel, *Vorlesungen über Rechtsphilosophie*, ed. Ilting (Stuttgart–Bad Cannstatt: Frommann-Holzboog, 1974), 4:530.

3. Ibid., 4:531.

4. This unrestricted generality comprises yet another ground for why law is situated within civil society rather than solely within the state. Because civil society has a global extension, exhibited in the self-expanding reach of market relations and the corresponding dissemination of classes and corporate interest groups, law can posit right most adequately without first being restricted by the boundary of political sovereignty, which always has a particular frontier demarcating its citizens from foreigners. In the first instance, law posits right as something applying to legal subjects in general, without yet distinguishing between citizens and noncitizens. Accordingly, the rules law mandates may just as well be promulgated in an international codification.

5. Hegel, *Philosophy of Right*, para. 210.

6. This distinction between objectivity as being an object of consciousness and as being universally actual is captured terminologically by Hegel in his rigorous use, respectively, of *"die Gegenständlichkeit"* and *"die Objectivität."*

7. In this vein, Hegel explains how the objective actuality of right consists in being an object of consciousness, in attaining the power to enforce itself as universally valid, and in becoming known to possess this universally effected validity. See Hegel, *Philosophy of Right*, para. 210.

8. Hegel, *Philosophy of Right*, para. 212; Hegel, *Vorlesungen über Rechtsphilosophie*, 3:648.

9. To the degree that education in the law is a prerequisite for knowing the law and competently participating as a legal subject, a just legal order must insure that all legal subjects are provided with either a sufficient legal training or access to those who have adequate legal knowledge, irrespective of any differences in wealth or any other factor that might condition their participation in legal affairs. This imperative becomes more determinate when the law attains its particular determination in view of the content of the rights it posits.

10. Hegel, *Vorlesungen über Rechtsphilosophie*, 5:645.

11. Ibid., 3:645.

12. This objectivity to knowing, as distinguished from objectivity in actuality, is what Hegel refers to as *die Gegenständlichkeit* as opposed to *die Objectivität.*

13. What is involved in enabling the authority of law to be recognizable in its expression in language is discussed in the next section. This account is not presupposed by the argument for why the language of law must not only be generally accessible, but also generally recognizable as authoritative.

14. Hegel, *Vorlesungen über Rechtsphilosophie*, 3:645.

15. This, of course, is the path suggested by, respectively, Hans Kelsen and H. L. A. Hart.

16. Hegel, *Vorlesungen über Rechtsphilosophie*, 3:646.

17. Although, systematically speaking, the only such rights that are already at hand are those of property, moral, family, and economic relations, the same feature will apply to the legalization of political rights as well as to the legalization of due process rights themselves.

18. Hegel, *Vorlesungen über Rechtsphilosophie*, 4:816.
19. Hegel, *Philosophy of Right*, para. 217.
20. Ibid., remark to para. 211.
21. Ibid., remark and addition to para. 211.
22. Konrad Zweigert and Hein Kötz, *Introduction to Comparative Law* (Oxford: Oxford University Press, 1987), 1:78.
23. Roberto Mangabeira Unger, *Law in Modern Society: Towards a Criticism of Social Theory* (New York: Free Press, 1976), 49–51.
24. Ibid.
25. Hegel, *Philosophy of Right*, remark to para. 211.
26. Ibid.
27. Plato, *Republic*, 405A-D. In the *Statesman*, Plato inveighs against law owing to the discrepancy between law's universality and the individuality of conduct (294B-C), yet admits that tyranny can only be avoided by uniting in a community governed by written laws (301E).
28. Zweigert and Kötz, *Introduction to Comparative Law*, 1:72.
29. See Foster, *The Political Philosophies of Plato and Hegel*, (Oxford: Oxford University Press, 1971), 116, for a discussion of this difference.
30. Hegel, *Philosophy of Right*, remark to para. 211.
31. Ibid., remark to para. 211; Hegel, *Vorlesungen über Rechtsphilosophie*, 4:535. See Zweigert and Kötz, *Introduction to Comparative Law*, 1:268–271, for a survey of how legal authorities in Great Britain and the United States have grappled with this dilemma..
32. Deconstructionists such as Derrida would have us believe that no abiding distinction can be drawn between the extralegal "violence" of founding a legal order and the application of law within an established legal system. This inability is because allegedly every application of law involves an act of interpretation whose discretionary judgment independently recreates law just as founders posit law independently of any fixed legal norms. (See Jacques Derrida, "Force of Law: The Mystical Foundations of Authority," *Cardozo Law Review*, 11: 5–6, [July/August 1990]: 940–944, 960–968.) Derrida ignores the fact that every application of law only counts as such on the basis of a common recognition of what comprises the body of law to be applied as well as who qualifies as authoritative judges to interpret its statutes and apply them to individual cases. H. L. A Hart makes this point in his criticism of "rule scepticism" in *The Concept of Law* (Oxford: Oxford University Press, 1982), 132–137. Those thinkers who would absolutize the hermeneutic situation always disregard this ineluctable feature of interpretation: that both interpreter and what is to be interpreted have a given content always beyond interpretation.
33. Hegel, *Philosophy of Right*, remark to para. 211.
34. Hegel, *Vorlesungen über Rechtsphilosophie*, 3:647.
35. Hegel, *Philosophy of Right*, para. 214.
36. This observation applies equally to the external dimensions of the rights of due process, which cannot be systematically introduced until the application of law in the courts is determined, as well as to the external

dimensions of political rights, which cannot be systematically introduced until the institutions of self-government have been conceived.

37. Hegel, *Philosophy of Right*, remark to para. 214.

38. Ibid., para. 214, remark to paragraph 214; Hegel, *Vorlesungen über Rechtsphilosophie*, 3:647, 651.

39. Hegel, *Vorlesungen über Rechtsphilosophie*, 4:812.

40. Kenley R. Dove has emphasized this global dimension of civil society in several recent talks delivered at meetings of the Society for Systematic Philosophy.

41. Properly speaking, the universal dimension of civil society is not merely global, given the possibility that humans may eventually colonize other worlds and that extraterrestrial rational agents inhabiting different worlds may well enter into the interdependent relations of the community of interest characterizing civil society. Although humans may never encounter extraterrestrial intelligent life and may never be able to have social intercourse with rational beings discovered beyond our solar system, it is conceivable that some aliens somewhere will participate in civil relationships transpiring between planets within or without their solar systems and within or without their galaxies.

42. Zweigert and Kötz, *Introduction to Comparative Law*, 1:105.

Chapter 5. The Form and Content of Law in Civil Society

1. G. W. F. Hegel, *Philosophy of Right*, trans. T. M. Knox (New York: Oxford University Press, 1967) para. 213; Hegel, *Vorlesungen über Rechtsphilosophie*, ed. Ilting (Stuttgart–Bad Cannstatt: Frommann-Holzboog, 1924), 3:649, 650, 651; 4:540.

2. Hegel, *Philosophy of Right*, para. 217.

3. Strictly speaking, persons may be male, female, hermaphroditic, or neuter, not simply because homo sapiens may be born with varying sexual identities, but because the concept of rational agency does not necessarily involve any particular form of gender differentiation. Although earthlings may not yet have encountered any rational creatures beyond themselves, the diversity with which terrestrial organisms reproduce themselves should indicate the possibilities that intelligent life might take.

4. Hegel, *Philosophy of Right*, para. 127.

5. Accordingly, Hegel points out that in civil society the taking ownership of unowned factors gets more and more supplanted by taking ownership through contract (ibid., para. 217, remark to para. 217, addition to para. 217).

6. Strict liability may enter in on the basis of entitlements grounded in the family and economic rights of individuals, which qualify the property entitlements they incorporate.

7. See Chapter 2, the section entitled "The Nonlegal Interpretation of Wrong."

8. By the same token, as will be shown, family and economic law will need to posit the right of individuals to have their household and market entitlements upheld at public expense in cases where neither malice, nor negligence, nor the particular property of some owner is involved in depriving individuals of the conditions to exercise their family and economic freedoms. Since it is the public rather than an individual that bears the burden for compensation in these cases, the principles of strict liability for nonmalicious wrong and no punishment without fault are not undermined but merely supplemented.

9. A systematic treatment of this prerogative depends upon a prior determination of the legal process, which itself presupposes an account of the form and content of law civil society.

10. See Hegel, *Philosophy of Right*, para. 127.

11. Peter P. Nicholson, "Hegel on Crime," *History of Political Thought*, 3:1 (Spring 1982): 119.

12. Aristotle, *Nicomachean Ethics*, bk. 5, chap. 4, 1131b–1132b.

13. Peter P. Nicholson, "Hegel on Crime," 119–120.

14. At one point in his *Vorlesungen über Rechtsphilosophie*, (4:550, 553), Hegel does suggest that punishment's nullification of the will of the criminal can involve taking hold of the criminal's will in the realm of representation and internally sublating the criminal's evil will. In this respect, he maintains, punishment can aim at improving the criminal. However, although the criminal may well entertain malicious purposes, they are malicious only insofar as the criminal understands that they are counter to right, and, in the context of civil society, illegal, but still independently chooses to follow whatever course of action he or she pursues. Consequently, whereas the illegal will can be countered from without through the constraint of punishment, the malicious purposes that guide it can only be countered from within by the malefactor. The latter is a moral concern beyond the scope of legal regulation. Hegel here forgets that moral improvement is always self-improvement.

15. Hegel mistakenly allows for the reduction of punishments in function of the improvement of the criminal, although he maintains that retribution must remain the supreme rationale for punishment (Hegel, *Vorlesungen über Rechtsphilosophie*, 4:553–554).

16. For a summary account of how Communist legal systems are marked by a tutelary conception of legality, see Zweigert and Kötz, *Introduction to Comparative Law*, (Oxford: Oxford University Press, 1987), 1:300–303, 320, 324–327, 332–333, 352–353, 355, 356.

17. Although Hegel maintains that retribution is the overriding rationale for punishment, he suggests that in relation to society, the standpoint of deterrence can affect sentencing (Hegel, *Vorlesungen über Rechtsphilosophie*, 4:554). This suggestion has greater plausibility than Hegel's accompanying assurance that the standpoint of rehabilitation be considered in determining punishment. For although deterrence cannot be the reason for punishing a criminal, the crime's significance as an injury to the legal fabric of civil society introduces the consideration that the punishment should fit the de-

gree of that injury, a fit that may well reflect a concern for its deterrent effect.

18. Hegel, *Vorlesungen über Rechtsphilosophie*, 3:662, 4:549.

19. Hegel, *Philosophy of Right*, para. 218, remark to para. 218, addition to para. 218; Hegel, *Vorlesungen über Rechtsphilosophie*, 3:661–662, 664, 4:551; Nicholson, "Hegel on Crime," 120.

20. Hegel, *Philosophy of Right*, para. 218; Hegel, *Vorlesungen über Rechtsphilosophie*, 3:662, 664.

21. Hegel, *Philosophy of Right*, remark to para. 218, addition to para. 218.

22. Ibid., para. 218, remark to para. 218, addition to para. 218; Hegel, *Vorlesungen über Rechtsphilosophie*, 4:554.

23. Once the rights and duties of citizens have been established, law, now situated within a constitutional framework and enacted through democratic legislation, will have to ensure that parents provide for the development of their children into autonomous citizens as well.

24. For a detailed account of economic freedom and the public measures that must be taken to uphold it, see Richard Dien Winfield, *The Just Economy*, (New York: Routledge, 1988), pt. 2.

25. Hegel analyzes these three factors under the rubric of the System of Needs, Corporations, and the Police. His analysis is marred by his conflation of estates with classes, which allows birthright and political privilege to have a foothold in economic affairs, in violation of the distinction between civil society and the state and reflecting a failure to free his thinking of the categories of feudal society, where privileges founded in hereditary rank determine at one and the same time the role of individuals in society and state. For a critique of Hegel's account, see Winfield, *Just Economy*, 149–156.

26. Roberto Mangabeira Unger, *The Critical Legal Studies Movement*, (Cambridge: Harvard University Press, 1986), 67.

27. Ibid., 67.

28. For a discussion of how the market generates barriers to the exercise of market freedom, see Winfield, *Just Economy*, 159–164.

29. For a further analysis of these limitations of economic interest group activity, see ibid., 174–182.

30. For a more complete discussion of these imperatives of public regulation of the market, see ibid., 183–229.

31. For a discussion of the perplexities of international law and international relations see "Political Freedom and Territorial Rights," chap. 16 in Winfield, *Freedom and Modernity* (Albany: State University of New York Press, 1991), 283–304.

32. Hegel, *Philosophy of Right*, remark to para. 211.

33. Hegel, *Vorlesungen über Rechtsphilosophie*, 3:654.

34. This point holds true, even if, as Hegel notes, the laws are no longer known by legal subjects in conditions of a developed civil society and state. (see ibid., 3:655). What counts is that the law is knowable and that individuals have access to whatever assistance is necessary to inform themselves of it.

35. By way of anticipation, it can be said that the legal code ought to

incorporate divisions for the law of due process regulating court procedures and the law of politics governing democratic political activity. Whereas the law of politics is determined in function of the concept of the institutions of political freedom, the law of due process is determined in respect to the concept of valid court procedures, which themselves can only be conceived in respect to how particular laws (first, those of property, family, and economic law) are applied to individual cases in civil society.

36. By way of anticipation, the same open completeness will apply to the codification of specifically legal rights of due process and of political rights.

37. These divisions will subsequently be supplemented by divisions corresponding to the rights of due process and of political freedom, which can be systematically determined when the court and the state are conceived.

38. Hegel, *Philosophy of Right*, para. 216; Hegel, *Vorlesungen über Rechtsphilosophie*, 3:657, 4:546.

39. Hegel, *Philosophy of Right*, addition to para. 214, remark to para. 216.

40. Ibid., remark to para. 215, addition to remark para. 215.

41. *The Nature of Law: Readings in Legal Philosophy*, edited by M. P. Golding (New York: Random House, 1966), 179.

42. Hart, H. L. A., *The Concept of Law* (Oxford: Oxford University Press, 1961), 121–150.

43. Ronald Dworkin, *Law's Empire* (Cambridge: Harvard University Press, 1986), 215–216, 254–258.

44. For further exploration of the self-inflicted collapse of skeptical denials of the universality of right, language, and conceptual thought, see Winfield, *Overcoming Foundations: Studies in Systematic Philosophy*, (New York: Columbia University Press, 1989), 77–89, 99–131.

45. Zweigert and Kötz, *Introduction to Comparative Law*, 1:66.

46. Ibid.

Chapter 6. The Legal Process

1. This is precisely how Hegel quite aptly characterizes the court. See G. W. F. Hegel, *Vorlesungen über Rechtsphilosophie*, ed. Ilting (Stuttgart–Bad Cannstatt: Frommann-Holzboog, 1974), 4:554.

2. In this vein, Hegel maintains that the historical genesis of courts and judges plays no role in determining the concept of the legal process. See G. W. F. Hegel, *Philosophy of Right*, trans. T. M. Knox (New York: Oxford University Press, 1967), remark to para. 219.

3. Ibid., remark to para. 219.

4. Ibid., para. 220. Admittedly, Hegel tends to limit this responsibility to criminal cases, but his discussion still provides the basic argument that applies to all types of violations of legally enforceable rights.

5. Hegel, *Vorlesungen über Rechtsphilosophie*, 3:670.

6. Hegel emphasizes the need for individuals to have knowledge of the law

as a precondition for being able to make use of the courts. See Hegel, *Philosophy of Right*, addition to para. 221; Hegel, *Vorlesungen über Rechtsphilosophie*, 3:672, 4:558.

7. So Hegel argues in behalf of a demarcation of the police and the court. See Hegel, *Vorlesungen über Rechtsphilosophie*, 4:575–576.

8. Ibid., 4:575.

9. Ibid., 4:554.

10. Hegel, *Philosophy of Right*, para. 224, addition to para. 224; Hegel, *Vorlesungen über Rechtsphilosophie* 3:675, 677–678.

11. Hegel, *Vorlesungen über Rechtsphilosophie*, 4:562–563.

12. For this reason, Hegel excludes deliberations of members of the court from the requirement of publicity. See Hegel, *Philosophy of Right*, remark to para. 224; Hegel, *Vorlesungen über Rechtsphilosophie*, 3:677.

13. Hegel, *Vorlesungen über Rechtsphilosophie*, 4:563–564.

14. Hegel, *Philosophy of Right*, para. 222.

15. Hegel, *Vorlesungen über Rechtsphilosophie*, 3:679.

16. Ibid., 3:679.

17. Hegel, *Philosophy of Right*, para. 227, addition to para. 227.

18. Hegel, *Vorlesungen ber Rechtsphilosophie*, 3:682–683.

19. Hegel, *Philosophy of Right*, addition to paragraph 227; Hegel, *Vorlesungen über Rechtsphilosophie*, 3:684.

20. Hegel, *Vorlesungen über Rechtsphilosophie*, 4:579.

21. Although Hegel acknowledges that confession does not have the final word, since false confessions are always possible, and admits that a jury should also certify the confession of the accused, (*Vorlesungen über Rechtsphilosophie*, 3:688), he still inadmissibly privileges confession by inconsistently maintaining that a jury trial has no right to enter in if the accused has confessed (ibid., 3:687).

22. The trial of James Earl Ray for the assassination of Martin Luther King provides a telling example of how allowing guilty pleas to put an end to court examinations of the facts of a case amounts to an abortion of legal justice.

23. Significantly, justifications of plea bargaining, whereby prosecutors reach an agreement with defenders to plead guilty to a lesser charge, are usually made on pragmatic grounds, such as that only with plea bargaining can overburdened courts and overburdened police achieve a modicum of successful prosecutions of the guilty. The argument does not rest upon any claim that those who plead guilty to a lesser charge are thereby providing irrefutable evidence of their guilt. Such a claim would be specious, particularly in light of how innocent defendants may well choose the lesser sentence in order to avoid the risk of being found guilty of a more serious crime.

24. David Luban, *Lawyers and Justice: An Ethical Study* (Princeton, NJ: Princeton University Press, 1988), 94.

25. Thomas Hobbes, *Leviathan*, ed. C. B. Macpherson (Harmondsworth, Eng.: Penguin Books, 1968), 269.

26. See Chapter 1 for a critique of liberal theory.

27. Robert Berman has raised this option in conversation as a more powerful reformulation of the Hobbesian objection.

28. So Luban argues, in homage to Hobbes. See Luban, *Lawyers and Justice*, 194–197.

29. Hegel, *Vorlesungen über Rechtsphilosophie*, 4:583.

30. However, exceptions are certainly possible, such as when a defendant has reason to protect someone else or to plead guilty to a lesser charge and avoid the risk of more severe punishment.

31. Hegel, *Vorlesungen über Rechtsphilosophie*, 4:584.

32. Luban, *Lawyers and Justice*, 194.

33. For this reason, Hegel is wrong to claim that the verdict of a jury is dubitable without the confession of the defendant. (Hegel, *Vorlesungen über Rechtsphilosophie*, 3:688.) Given the fallibility of confession, it would be more correct to say that the verdict is just as dubitable with or without the confession but not necessarily reasonably dubitable in either case.

34. Luban, *Lawyers and Justice*, 193.

35. Ibid., 193–194.

36. For this reason, Hegel criticizes the British legal system for leaving the determination of the charge to the arbitrariness of the plaintiff, even when the court discovers that the charge is incorrect. See Hegel, *Philosophy of Right*, remark to para. 225.

37. Luban, *Lawyers and Justice*, 94.

38. Hegel, *Philosophy of Right*, para. 227.

39. Hegel, *Vorlesungen über Rechtsphilosophie*, 4:559.

40. Hegel, *Philosophy of Right*, para. 226.

41. Hegel suggests that the justification of jury trials chiefly revolves around the separate execution of the two functions of the court. (Hegel, *Vorlesungen über Rechtsphilosophie*, 4:577). However, although the two functions are separately executed, their separate execution does not necessarily depend upon separate executors. Although different groups of individuals may perform each function separately, the same individuals may just as well perform each in succession.

42. Hegel, *Philosophy of Right*, para. 223.

43. As Robert Berman points out, John Rawls's characterization of impure proceduralism captures that aspect of the legal process that raises the issue of equity.

44. Hegel, *Vorlesungen über Rechtsphilosophie*, 3:674.

45. Ibid., 4:560.

46. Hegel, *Philosophy of Right*, remark to para. 223; Hegel, *Vorlesungen über Rechtsphilosophie*, 4:561.

47. See Zweigert and Kötz, *Introduction to Comparative Law*, (Oxford; Oxford University Press, 1987), 1:94–198, 206.

48. Kant, *The Metaphysics of Morals*, trans. Mary Gregor (New York; Cambridge University press, 1991), 59, Ak. 234.

49. Hegel emphasizes the importance of this freedom to choose whether

to have an equity settlement. See Hegel, *Vorlesungen über Rechtsphilosophie*, 4:561.

50. Oakeshott, *On Human Conduct* (Oxford: Oxford University Press, 1975),132–133.

51. Zweigert and Kötz, *Introduction to Comparative Law*, 2:376.

52. Hegel, *Philosophy of Right*, para. 225.

53. Hegel, *Vorlesungen über Rechtsphilosophie*, 3:678.

54. Oakeshott, *On Human Conduct*, 134.

55. Hegel, *Vorlesungen über Rechtsphilosophie*, 4:565.

56. Oakeshott, *On Human Conduct*, 133.

57. Ibid., 136.

58. Ibid., 134.

59. Hegel, *Vorlesungen ber Rechtsphilosophie*, 4:567.

60. Ibid., 4:566.

61. Alexis de Tocqueville, *De la Démocratie en Amérique* (Paris: Garnier-Flammarion, 1981), 1:371–378.

62. It could be argued against them all that any political justifications of "democratizations" of the legal system conflate the freedoms of politics with the freedoms of civil society. Similar confusions afflict arguments in behalf of economic democracy. In each case, the prerogatives of political freedom are made supreme, to the potential exclusion of the other modes of self-determination. The ultimate result of this imposition is the reign of absolute freedom and terror, where the total politicization of all relations sacrifices all nonpolitical domains of autonomy to the iron will of collective decision making.

63. Hegel, *Vorlesungen über Rechtsphilosophie*, 4:569.

64. Ibid., 4:570.

65. Ibid., 4:571.

66. Ibid., 3:679.

67. Ibid., 3:678.

68. Hegel, *Philosophy of Right*, addition to para. 227.

69. Ibid., para. 228; *Vorlesungen über Rechtsphilosophie*, 3:686.

70. Hegel, *Vorlesungen über Rechtsphilosophie*, 3:683.

71. Ibid., 4:578–579.

72. Hegel, *Philosophy of Right*, para. 228.

73. For a detailed critique of Hegel's appeal to estates, see Winfield, *The Just Economy*, (New York: Routledge, 1988), 149–156.

74. Hegel, *Philosophy of Right*, remark to para. 228; Hegel, *Vorlesungen über Rechtsphilosophie*, 3:687.

75. Hegel, *Vorlesungen über Rechtsphilosophie*, 4:581.

76. Ibid., 4:577.

77. Ibid.

78. Ibid., 4:576.

79. At one point, Hegel himself admits as much, acknowledging that the role of deciding the facts of the case can be given to a judge, although it is not

something exclusive to him in his capacity as judge, since any educated individual is capable of performing this function (ibid., 4:572).

80. Ibid., 4;581.

81. Ibid., 4:583.

82. Ibid., 4:574.

83. Peter P. Nicholson argues this connection at length, drawing upon Hegel's differentiation between nonmalicious and malicious wrong. See Nicholson, "Hegel on Crime," *History of Political Thought* 3:1 (Spring 1982). The following discussion largely draws upon Nicholson's argument and the distinctions of Hegel on which Nicholson relies.

84. Nicholson, "Hegel on Crime," 118; Aristotle, *Nicomachean Ethics*, bk. 5, chap. 4, 1131b–1132b.

85. Peter P. Nicholson outlines the following differences and attempts to trace them back to the distinction Hegel draws between nonmalicious and malicious wrong. See Nicholson, "Hegel on Crime."

86. Hegel, *Philosophy of Right*, addition to para. 130.

87. Ibid., para. 220.

88. Nicholson, "Hegel on Crime," 114.

89. Zweigert and Kötz, *Introduction to Comparative Law*, 1:284.

90. de Tocqueville, *De la Démocratie*, 1:375–378.

91. To determine whether either deserves *exclusive* adoption requires assessing all other possible alternatives, a task that goes beyond the adversary system/inquisitorial system controversy. Raymond A. Belliotti emphasizes this requirement in his survey of arguments pro and con regarding the adversary system in "Our Adversary System: In Search of a Foundation," *Canadian Journal of Law and Jurisprudence*, 1:1 (January 1988): 19–34.

92. What is here termed the "inquisitorial" system is elsewhere labeled the "civil" system in distinction to the adversary system. However, since these opposing systems of trial practice are not defined in terms of differing connections to civil society or the contrast between "civil" and criminal law, the "inquisitorial" label is less confusing. Zweigert and Kötz label the "inquisitorial" system that of "civil" law because of their fixation upon the historical examples in which inquisitorial trial practice goes hand in hand with codified law and a comparative absence of jury trials (Zweigert and Kötz, *Introduction to Comparative Law*, 1:264–284). Since, however, these historical connections are contingent ties that have no essential role in the "inquisitorial" system, it is all the more important to abandon the "civil" label that Zweigert and Kötz, among others, apply.

93. Luban, *Lawyers and Justice*, 57.

94. Zweigert and Kötz, *Introduction to Comparative Law*, 1:280–284.

95. Ibid., 1:281.

96. Ibid.

97. Ibid., 1:282.

98. Ibid., 1:282–283.

99. Ibid.

100. David Luban makes this point but restricts his evaluation of the adversary system to its ramifications within court adjudication, rationalizing that any problems in that sphere will only be intensified outside it (Luban, *Lawyers and Justice*, 57–58). However, the sphere at stake remains the same: legality in civil society, whose imperatives extend equally within and without the courtroom.

101. David Luban critically discusses this characterization of the adversary system at length in *Lawyers and Justice*, 50–66.

102. In the course of advancing a pragmatic justification of the adversary system, David Luban argues that the principle of nonaccountability is false because partisanship must be restricted by holding lawyers morally accountable for both the ends they advance and the instruments they employ (see ibid., 56ff.). Given, however, the inherent subjectivity of moral reflection, moral accountability cannot set firm restrictions upon court behavior. As we shall see, what imposes limits upon partisanship are the enforceable rights of individuals in civil society. Then the question becomes whether the resulting restrictions upon partisanship in legal proceedings leave the truncated "adversary" system any different from its inquisitorial counterpart.

103. Ibid., 75.

104. See ibid., 87–92, for additional related criticisms of these justifications.

105. See chap. 10 of John Locke's *The Second Treatise on Government* (Indianapolis: Bobbs-Merrill, 1952), 73.

106. Luban, *Lawyers and Justice*, 58.

107. Ibid., 59.

108. An exclusionary rule that bars the introduction of evidence that is illegally obtained may serve as a deterrent to improper searches, but it equally obstructs the right of all parties to a trial to have an objective investigation of the facts of a case. As long as stiff penalties are mandated and rigorously enforced for illegally obtaining evidence, the aims of the exclusionary rule can be served without undermining the factual determinations that must be made to prepare a case for subsumption under the law.

109. Luban, *Lawyers and Justice*, 62.

110. Ibid., 60–61.

111. Ibid., 61.

112. Luban mistakenly identifies it in these political terms, while also setting it under the "criminal defense paradigm," neglecting the full breadth of civil cases in which private parties face public authority. See ibid., 63.

113. Ibid., 63–64.

114. Ibid., 69.

115. Ibid., 71–74.

116. Consequently, even if Fuller and Randall are correct in thinking that a neutral judge cannot effectively personify all sides in a case while retaining impartiality, this hardly means that adversarial advocacy will better reveal the truth. See Lon Fuller and John D. Randall, "Professional Responsibility:

Report of the Joint Conference of the ABA-AALS," *ABA Journal* 44 (1958): 1160 (cited in Luban, *Lawyers and Justice*, 71).

117. However, neither the exclusionary rule nor the "right" against self-incrimination are valid indexes of this limit to the truth-finding imperative of trials, as Monroe Freedman maintains in *Lawyers' Ethics in an Adversary System* (Indianapolis: Bobbs-Merrill, 1975), 3–4 (cited in Luban, *Lawyers and Justice*, 74). As prior argument has shown, neither fixtures of U.S. legal practice are systematically mandated by law in civil society.

118. Luban, *Lawyers and Justice*, 76.

119. See Luban's parallel critique of the defense of the adversary system as a reliable system of checks-and-balances (ibid., 78-79).

120. Ibid., 85.

121. Ibid., 85–87.

122. Charles Fried ignores this side of partisan advocacy in extolling its alleged promotion of fraternal virtue. See Charles Fried, "The Lawyer as Friend: The Moral Foundations of the Lawyer-Client Relation," *Yale Law Journal* 85 (1976): 1068–1073 (cited and similarly critiqued in Luban, *Lawyers and Justice*, 82).

123. Luban, *Lawyers and Justice*, 92.

124. Luban maintains that inquisitorial trials will be impractical under common law because the greater burdens of legal research in uncovering judicial precedent make it unwieldy for judges to take on the lion's share of case preparation (ibid., 101). It can be questioned why courts need be less able to carry the expense and effort of such research than clients and their lawyers. Since, however, legal right mandates codification, this point is moot when it comes to evaluating the inquisitorial system. For, as Luban admits, (ibid., 101), the relative ease of researching a legal code well suits an inquisitorial system.

125. This last option, which, historically, happens to be practiced in inquisitorial systems but not in adversary systems, is mandated by due process and should therefore apply whether or not inquisitorial or adversary methods are employed.

126. Luban lists the above features in describing contemporary German legal practice. See Luban, *Lawyers and Justice*, 94.

127. Zweigert and Kötz, *Introduction to Comparative Law*, 1:134.

128. Ibid., 1:131.

129. Ibid., 1:134.

130. Luban intimates this danger. See Luban, *Lawyers and Justice* 102.

131. Luban describes how this dual independence functions in the context of the German legal system. See ibid., 96.

132. Zweigert and Kötz, *Introduction to Comparative Law*, 1:132.

133. Luban, *Lawyers and Justice*, 97.

134. Luban makes this accusation. See ibid., 100.

135. Ibid., 99.

136. This abiding independence of participating lawyers can counteract

encroachments on defendants' rights, such as Tomlinson complains has occurred in the inquisitorial system in France, where allegedly the fact-finding of the examining magistrate has become subordinate to the prosecutor and police. See Edward Tomlinson, "Nonadversarial Justice: The French Experience," *Maryland Law Review* 42 (1983): 150–195 (cited in Luban, *Lawyers and Justice,* 99).

137. Luban, *Lawyers and Justice,* 99.

138. Luban raises these objections. See ibid., 100.

139. Luban suggests that it does. See ibid., 101.

140. Luban endorses this suspicion, although it contradicts his merely pragmatic acceptance of the adversary system unless popular control is itself merely pragmatically desirable (see ibid., 103). Belliotti rightly criticizes Luban for artificially truncating the debate by ignoring other means of limiting state power. See Belliotti, "Our Adversary System," 33–34.

141. As Belliotti observes, the outcome of any debate between the adversary and inquisitorial systems cannot provide an absolute justification of either unless the absence of any other equal or better alternatives can be established. See Belliotti, "Our Adversary System," 34.

142. Hegel, for his part, embraces the inquisitorial system, with the qualification that he combines it with mandatory jury trials. He accordingly insists that the role of a lawyer in a jury trial is not to function as a defender but as someone leading the examination of witnesses, where the lawyer only brings out the witnesses for questioning by the jurors (Hegel, *Vorlesungen über Rechtsphilosophie,* 4:573). Hegel charges the judge, meanwhile, with leading the investigation of the facts of the case, knowing the law, and subsuming the case under it (*Vorlesungen über Rechtsphilosophie,* 4:574).

143. Kant, *Metaphysics of Morals,* 139–140, Ak. 330.

144. Hobbes, *Leviathan,* 269, 353.

145. Kant considers such punishments admissible, in conformity with his treatment of the criminal as literally an outlaw, stripped of rights. See Kant, *Metaphysics of Morals,* 139–140, Ak. 330.

146. For discussions of constitutionality, legislation, and the division of powers, see Richard Dien Winfield, *Reason and Justice* (Albany: State University of New York Press, 1988), 251–282, 288–297; Winfield, *Overcoming Foundations* (New York: Columbia University Press, 1989), 217–269, 282–291; and Winfield, *Freedom and Modernity* (Albany: State University of New York Press, 1991), 261–282.

147. See Winfield, *Freedom and Modernity,* 283–301, for a discussion of the basic issues underlying international law.

Index